HOW TO BE AN EPICUREAN

THE ANCIENT ART OF LIVING WELL

CATHERINE WILSON

BASIC BOOKS

New York

Basic Books
Hachette Book Group
1290 Avenue of the Americas, New York, NY 10104
www.basicbooks.com

Printed in the United States of America

Originally published in 2019 by HarperCollins Publishers in the United Kingdom

First US Edition: September 2019

Published by Basic Books, an imprint of Perseus Books, LLC, a subsidiary of Hachette Book Group, Inc. The Basic Books name and logo is a trademark of the Hachette Book Group.

The Hachette Speakers Bureau provides a wide range of authors for speaking events. To find out more, go to www.hachettespeakersbureau.com or call (866) 376-6591.

The publisher is not responsible for websites (or their content) that are not owned by the publisher.

Library of Congress Cataloging-in-Publication Data has been applied for.

ISBNs: 978-1-5416-7263-5 (hardcover), 978-1-5416-7262-8 (ebook)

LSC-C

10 9 8 7 6 5 4 3 2 1

CONTENTS

PART II: LIVING WELL AND LIVING JUSTLY

PREFACE

Philosophy wears garments of many colours and textures. It can stitch together intricate analysis or pretentious baffle-gab, deep insight or pseudo-profundity, impartial advice or personal prejudice. It shows up, in flashy or drab form, not only in the lecture rooms of universities but in the New Age section of your local bookshop, shelved next to books about ESP and meditation. Regardless of its patchwork character, philosophy asks you to try to think for yourself, logically and coherently, to create order from chaos. You use ideas and frameworks developed by others, especially the great philosophers of the past, as scaffolding. But ultimately, you make – and use – your own system of the world in deciding what to believe, what to do and what to hope for.

My aim in this book is to build you a piece of scaffolding by introducing you to what, to me, is the most interesting and relevant of the ancient philosophical systems: Epicureanism, a 'theory of everything' originating in the observations and ideas of the 3rd-century-BCE Athenian philosopher Epicurus and set into Latin verse by his 1st-century-BCE Roman follower, Titus Carus Lucretius. Although the world has changed since Epicurus wrote and lectured, the issues of money, love, family and politics that he dealt with remain with us in new forms. The Epicurean perspective remains, to my mind, relevant and valuable.

Epicureanism was one of the five major schools of ancient Greek and Roman philosophy, existing alongside – and competing for adherents with – Platonism, Stoicism, Scepticism and Aristotelianism. Unlike the city-based Platonists and Stoics, Epicurus had decided to 'live apart' with his followers. His philosophical school was set in a garden (actually a grove), usually considered to have been located outside the city walls, where philosophy was discussed, meals were taken together, and books and letters were written.

Most of Epicurus's original writings were lost. The largest known collection of his and his followers' writings, located in the town of Herculaneum near Naples, was buried in the ash and lava of the eruption of Mount Vesuvius in 79 CE. But Lucretius had seen and made use of them more than a century earlier, and several of Epicurus's philosophical letters and collections of sayings, as well as the reports of ancient commentators, survived.

Marcus Tullius Cicero, Lucretius's Roman contemporary, took an interest in Epicureanism, though he criticised it heavily. His dialogues on religion and moral philosophy show how Epicureanism stacked up against its rival Stoicism, at least from Cicero's point of view. Largely but not wholly lost to medieval and Renaissance readers, Epicurean philosophy was revived in the 17th century, when it exercised a significant influence on moral and political philosophy, as well as on cosmology, chemistry and physics. The great utilitarian social reformers of 19th-century Britain, as well as the framers of the United States Constitution, paid homage to the Epicurean ideal of human welfare. And Lucretius's Epicurean poem, *On the Nature of*

Things, at first admired mainly for its elegant Latin, came to be considered a model for the vivid and memorable communication of abstract scientific ideas. At the same time, as you will see in what follows, Epicureanism had certain features that shocked, or at least unsettled, many who encountered it.

Before I start, more about me: as a lecturer, I have taught philosophy in the US, Britain, Canada and Germany. As a researcher I have worked in archives and libraries, published books and articles, and engaged in controversies with other academics. Many of my writings focus on the physical and life sciences of the 17th and 18th centuries, and especially on the concept of the microworld of subvisible organisms and material particles. But all along, thanks to early exposure as a teenager through volunteer activities and work camps, I have been interested in the problems of warfare, poverty and social justice. Both sets of interests are reflected in this book, which is addressed to some of the problems of modernity, both theoretical and practical, as they face us in contemporary life.

Like most readers, I am concerned about the array of political and economic problems affecting us and our children and causing us anxiety even when we live in conditions of affluence. There is increasing economic inequality, fostering resentment and violence; the corruption of democratic processes on a mass scale; the existential threats posed by climate change and nuclear, chemical and biological weapons; the depletion of environmental resources, including soil and water; the loss of plant and animal species, and the toxification of our air and our oceans.

The modern economy uses vast quantities of energy from oil and gas (and from the atom) to transform oil and other raw materials into consumer products, only a few of which make our lives better. The rest stuffs and fattens our closets and drawers

3

and piles up as waste in landfills. And it does not make us happy. Mood disturbances, especially depression, afflict large segments of the population, and many people drink too much alcohol or are addicted to stimulants or tranquillisers. Over one-third of Americans are 'completely inactive', and sleep disturbances from artificial light as well as immune dysregulation arise from lack of exposure to natural sunlight. 'In effect,' as one observer comments, 'humans have dragged a body with a long hominid history into an overfed, malnourished, sedentary, sunlight-deficient, sleep-deprived, competitive, inequitable and socially isolating environment with dire consequences.' We live longer than most of our ancestors but in a sicklier fashion. And from every pain or deprivation, somebody benefits. Pharmaceutical manufacturers benefit from our sugar-induced diabetes and our mental-health problems; oil companies from the destruction of wilderness and poisoning of the atmosphere; the chemicals industry and their stockholders from the use of plastics; the automobile industry from the absence of public transportation; and the prison industry from the desperation and violence that characterise the poorest neighbourhoods.

At the same time, we face problems in our private lives that reflect the age-old human condition, intensified by the social changes of the last fifty to one hundred years. The stresses of urban life, the monotony of suburban life, bad jobs and bad bosses, sexual predation and confusion affect almost all of us.

Tinkering around the edges of our problems with scented candles, new exercise routines and productivity apps isn't going to help much in the long-run, and no philosopher who is honest about it can give you a formula for being happy – certainly not for being happy all the time. Nevertheless, philosophy can point the way to the sources of satisfaction that are available to almost every human being and to strategies for facing off against the major threats to human happiness. These threats lie in wait for us in the form of outsized ambitions, fear of failure and feelings of futility. The history of philosophy can also help us to see the difference between what philosophers call the necessary and the contingent, or accidental in our historical and social conditions, and to see how the moral commitments of individuals have made a positive difference.

In this book, I'll explain how the ancient Epicureans saw the world and how a present-day Epicurean sees it. At the same time, I'll try to be honest and objective. Epicureanism was always a controversial philosophy, and it needs rethinking in some respects. Philosophers have their own irrational enthusiasms, and their views should never be accepted on faith without critical scrutiny. As far as that's concerned, I expect readers to roll their eyes at some of my opinions. In the end, you may find the Epicurean system as I present it here compelling and useful in working out your own ideas about how to live. Or you may find it offputting and see in its very problems helpful directions for living in a different way. In any case, real Epicureanism is probably considerably different from what you might have thought.

As reported by Lucretius:

[Epicurus] saw that almost everything that necessity demands for subsistence had already been provided for mortals ... he saw, too, that they possessed power, with wealth, honour and glory, and took pride in the good reputation of their children; and yet he found that, notwithstanding this prosperity, all of them privately had hearts ranked with anxiety ...

The Epicureans believed that most people have the wrong conception of the nature of the universe and their place in it. They wanted to replace indoctrination and wishful thinking with respect for reality. They sought to uncover the real sources of joy and misery in our finite lives and to balance the ethical treatment of others with our own self-interest. This required attention to opportunities for 'choice and avoidance' in everyday life. Three of Epicurus's most famous (also his most infamous) teachings were: first, everything that exists, including the human mind, is composed of material atoms; second, if a God or gods exist, it or they did not create our world, and it or they do not care about humanity; and third, there is no life after death and no other world to go to.

From these three basic and interrelated claims – the material nature of everything, including the human individual, the absence of divine oversight of the world and the finality of death – the Epicureans worked out a system covering both the natural world and the human world. They tried, ambitiously, though not always convincingly, to explain the origins of the cosmos, the causes of volcanoes and earthquakes, the evolution of life and the origins of war, poverty, dominion and servitude, appealing only to physical processes and human inventions and decisions. They explained what morality and justice are all about and warned of the dangers of belligerent and kleptocratic rulers. They made suggestions as to how to live with less fear and regret and what attitude to take in the face of adversity. Unlike their main philosophical rivals, the Stoics, they did not believe the mind is all-powerful in the face of adversity or that we should strive to repress our emotions, griefs and passions. Their moral philosophy is relational rather than individualistic. And unlike the other, more influential schools of ancient philosophy, especially the Platonic and the Aristotelian, the Epicureans welcomed women into the sect.

Central to their understanding and to their views on social equality was their distinction between nature and what they termed 'convention'. By nature they meant the realm of living things – what we would call the plant and animal kingdoms – along with light and fire, the varied landscapes and waterscapes of our planet, and its celestial objects, the sun, moon and stars. Nature, they recognised, presents an ever-changing spectacle, but it is in many ways predictable. The seasons come around on a regular basis, and animals produce offspring that resemble them from generation to generation. Fire can be counted upon to burn dry straw.

By convention the Epicureans meant perceptions, attitudes and beliefs dependent on our specifically human constitution and reflected in our categories and the words we use. Epicurus's Greek forerunner, the philosopher Democritus, stated: 'By convention sweet, by convention bitter, by convention hot, by convention cold, by convention colour: but in reality, atoms and the void.' The sweetness of honey and the bitterness of rocket depend on our taste receptors, and colours, too, are perceived differently by different animal species and even by different individual humans. Poverty and marriage are not found in nature; they are understood differently by different groups of humans and have different implications, depending on where you are and what group you identify with.

The distinction between nature and convention helps to break down egocentrism and speciesism. My perceptions don't have any special claim to objectivity, and my preferences – indeed, human desires in general – don't deserve automatic priority over the preferences of other people and animals. The nature–convention distinction is also important for taking a critical perspective on politics, economics and social relations. In adolescence, most of us come to a point where we question the rules and structures that we have to obey and live within. Some people retain this inquisitive, even rebellious spirit for their entire lives; others decide in time that there are good reasons why things are organised and administered the way they are, or that acceptance and conformity are necessary for getting ahead in life. The Epicurean is acutely aware that our institutions and practices – our schools, law courts, police systems and government bodies – along with our ways of making things and selling them, and our expectations from marriage and family life, are conventional. *We* have decided that they are to take on the forms they have. At the same time, to refer to 'our' decisions is to gloss over the fact that the decisions that actually shape our lives are rarely made by the same people whose lives are shaped by them.

Many customs and policies that are purely conventional are assumed to be based in nature and treated as just, beneficial and unchangeable. Some examples, which I will discuss later in the book, include our supposedly natural selfishness and our supposedly unlimited desire for material goods. The assumption that acquisitiveness is a primary human drive provides the rationale for the way we organise and reward work. The supposed natural differences between men and women, in respect of their abilities, temperaments and interests, provides the rationale for giving women less of many of the things that men enjoy in greater abundance, especially social freedom and the opportunity to develop their talents and contribute to how the world is going to look and operate.

Although I have found Epicurean philosophy to be a rich source of ideas for thinking about nature, society, and personal life, the decision to write about Epicureanism for a broader readership presented a challenge nothing like the ones I was used to in my professional role.

First, in the more than 2,000 years since Epicurus founded his school of philosophy, the world has undergone a series of technological and political upheavals. We have experienced the Industrial Revolution, the agricultural revolution, the rise of global capitalism and factory labour, and the Internet revolution. We have an understanding of physics, chemistry, biology, astronomy, medicine, mathematics, engineering, computing and the social sciences that has enabled us to develop and transform our environment and to accumulate and share experiences in ways that could never have been foreseen. We can observe and communicate at the speed of light with people on the other side of the world. Could the ideas of an ancient philosopher from a time when civilisation, though not the world itself, was young, and when what expert knowledge there was lay in the hands of a small elite, really have any relevance today?

Second, Epicureanism is an optimistic philosophy, but it is not the intellectual equivalent of comfort food. Lucretius described Epicurus's world view as bitter medicine that he aimed to sweeten through the sensuous imagery of his poetry. The Epicureans were concerned with how to think clearly and objectively about the world and about our social and political relations with one another, and they did not shrink from stating inconvenient truths. Could modern readers be persuaded that it was worth taking the medicine?

Third, the words 'Epicure' and 'Epicurean' are associated with unbridled consumption and high living. If you think visually, the first image that comes to mind might be that of a dainty, emaciated aristocrat, fussing over his wine cellar, or that of a fat, jowly, solitary diner with a voluminous napkin tucked under his chin, tackling an enormous roast. You probably weren't thinking of a middle-aged woman who owns a bicycle and whose refrigerator at the moment contains only a few wilting green onions and half a jar of marmalade.

In fact, Epicurus did consider pleasure, including pleasure in food and drink, to be not only the main motive of our actions but also the supreme good. As he put it:

> Pleasure is our first and kindred good. It is the starting point of every choice and of every aversion, and to it we come back, inasmuch as we make feeling the rule by which to judge of every good thing.

This may strike you as an unacceptably frivolous and selfish claim. What would the world look like if everybody forgot about calories, the family, sales goals, deadlines, grades, the nation, truth, honour and responsibility and instead went all-out in the pursuit of pleasure? What about the sexually transmitted diseases, overdoses and bankruptcies that would inevitably follow? What about the feelings, pleasures and choices of the sadist? And isn't the pursuit of pleasure expensive and ecologically irresponsible?

Let me reassure you that real Epicureanism is neither frivolous nor dangerous to health, nor a threat to other people. Epicurus himself pointed out that the direct pursuit of pleasurable sensations is usually self-defeating. At the same time, he stated clearly that the best life is one free of deprivations, starting with freedom from hunger, thirst and cold, and freedom from persistent fears and anxieties. Living well requires friends to entertain and comfort us and curiosity about nature and how the world works. It doesn't require stupendous achievement or large outlays of cash. And life can be and feel significant even without religious faith in the usual sense. Although it might seem surprising in light of the many attacks from medieval and early-modern Western theologians on Epicureanism for its athe-istic framework, the Epicurean conception of the good and meaningful life can even be found in the Jewish and Christian bibles. Ecclesiastes 8:15 says, 'Then I commended mirth, because a man hath no better thing under the sun, than to eat, and to drink, and to be merry.' Isaiah 22:13 says, 'Let us eat and drink; for tomorrow we shall die.'

Although Epicureanism is a way of life, this is not a lifestyle book in the usual sense. I start off with a generous helping of Epicurean physics, the theory of nature and history, with the Epicurean theory of everything. My contention is that ethical and political values are grounded in particular ways of seeing the world, about which we are normally unreflective. Philosophy brings these assumptions to the surface and makes them explicit so that they can be examined, and refined or discarded. Our choices should flow spontaneously from our examined convic-tions without our having to take on board and remember specific rules, including rules for living. I can't solve for my readers all or even many of the problems of modern life, but I hope my book will help you to acquire a framework for living, not only comfortably and happily, as far as possible, but in a responsible and meaningful way.

NOTE ON THE TEXT

Most of Epicurus's original writings have been lost, though the collection destroyed in the eruption of Mount Vesuvius in 79 CE has recently been partially rescued and partially restored to legibility. I've drawn on the most available of Epicurus's letters and sayings and on Lucretius's poem, *On the Nature of Things*, based on Epicurus's still mostly unreconstructed book *On Nature*. Bibliographical information is found at the end, along with suggestions for further reading.

PART I

How the Epicurean Sees the World

1

BACK TO BASICS

*The totality is made up of bodies and void ... Beyond these
two things nothing can be conceived ... Among bodies,
some are compounds, and some are those things from which
compounds have been made. And these are atomic
and unchangeable ...*

Epicurus

*There are certain particles whose concurrences, movements,
order, position and shapes produce fires; different
combinations of them form things of different nature, but
they themselves are unlike fire or any other thing ...*

Lucretius

Let's start with a set of questions – large ones, with significant implications – to which the Epicurean has a definite answer. Is there anything completely indestructible and permanent in the universe? If so, what is it? And why does the Epicurean answer to such an abstract question matter?

In thinking about endurance, we can immediately rule out tables and chairs, houses and skyscrapers, pens and pencils, and all other objects that human beings fabricate. All of these items have finite useful lives ranging from a few months to a few thousand years. Any of these items can be broken up by taking a crowbar or a wrecking ball to it, or just by snapping it in two in the case of pens and pencils. Left to themselves, over hundreds or thousands of years, each of these items will crumble into dust. Plastic bags, we have learned to our dismay, will persist for an astonishingly long time, perhaps a thousand years in landfills, but eventually they, too, will be broken down by light or heat, or by chemicals or micro-organisms.

Very well, what about enormous natural objects like mountains or the ocean? They are not so easy to destroy, but enough nuclear weapons or a very large asteroid could flatten the

Himalayas. And in time – in hundreds of millions or several billion years – all life on our planet will have long been extinct. The earth will be consumed by the sun within 5 billion years, and our galaxy will collapse.

What, then, about the chemical elements – hydrogen, carbon, uranium and so on? There are many competing scenarios for the end of the universe as we know it and the disappearance of every galaxy, but in all of them the chemical elements, too, will eventually vanish.

Even time and space, and the so-called elementary particles, the quarks and gluons and bosons, will cease to exist, according to current theory.

But, surely something must continue to exist! The universe can never wind down into *nothing* ... zero ... total annihilation ...?

THE EPICUREAN ATOM

The ancient Epicureans argued that everything in our experience is perishable and will someday perish. But once *something* exists, they reasoned, it cannot just become *nothing*. Correspondingly, the entire universe could not have come out of nothing. It follows that the universe must have emerged from *something* and that something will always exist, no matter how broken up the objects of experience come to be.

If they were right – and let's go along with their reasoning – after the destruction of every man-made object, every geographical feature, every star and planet, and every chemical element, and after the disappearance of time and space, *something* must be left from which a new universe could be rebuilt.

From the time that human beings began to philosophise, many came to the conclusion that the eternal something that existed before the universe ever appeared and that can maintain it or even outlast it must be intelligent and creative – a Mind with a Plan. Creation stories take many different forms, but they have in common the idea that there must have been a definite beginning to the world and that it was brought into being for some purpose by its Creator. Human beings were the special concern of this powerful entity, and the rest of the universe was constructed according to the needs and characteristics of human beings and the grand plan of the Creator for them.

Epicurus rejected these assumptions. He maintained to the contrary that the elements of the universe are eternal and uncreated. There is no ruling mind or master plan involving them. His reasoning begins from the idea of destruction rather than from the idea of construction.

Destruction occurs when the parts of a thing, whether a boulder, or a house, or an animal body, are separated from one another by tearing, grinding, smashing, chopping, wearing away or being exploded. The truly indestructible and permanent things that remain after all such operations are the 'atoms' – in Greek, the 'uncuttables'. Epicurean atoms are the ancestors of the modern scientific concept of the atom, but somewhat differently imagined. They are located and move in the void, the empty space separating visible objects and constituting the tiny gaps between the atoms of different shapes and sizes within objects. Apart from the atoms and the void in which they move and collect, sticking together and interweaving, there is nothing.

These atoms, Epicurus supposed, are far too small to be seen by human eyes. But the existence of tiny indestructible particles composing everything was suggested not only by the reasoning just described but by common observations. 'A finger ring,' says Lucretius, 'is worn thin on the inside; the fall of water drop by drop hollows a stone; we see the stone pavements of streets worn away by the feet of the crowd.' The atoms were thought to resemble the dust motes that can be seen drifting in a ray of light coming in through a window. According to Epicurus, they have different shapes and sizes, but are devoid of colour, taste and scent. They can move in all directions and have no tendencies except the tendency to fall downwards, and the ability to rebound from one other, and to become entangled with other atoms to form physical objects of perceptible sizes. Frequently, an atom 'swerves' in an unpredictable fashion. If they didn't, they'd all end up in a pile at the 'bottom' of the world.

The Epicureans theorised that, given sufficient time, the atoms would fall into stable patterns. They would form multiple worlds, or 'cosmoi', each with its own plants and animals, its own stars and sun. Such worlds were, they thought, constantly coming into being and breaking up, furnishing the material for recycling into new worlds.

'The same atoms,' Lucretius points out, 'constitute sky, sea, lands, rivers and sun: the same compose crops, trees and animals.' But if the atoms have no qualities other than size, shape and motion, how can they give rise to our noisy, colourful, scented, textured world? The answer, he explains, is that combinations and arrangements of atoms can take on qualities they do not possess individually. He employs the analogy of letters and words.

The 26 letters of the Roman alphabet can be combined into at least 100,000 meaningful words of the English language. Some linguists maintain that there are up to 1,000,000 words in English, though nobody's vocabulary could have that breadth. And from even 100,000 words, millions of intelligible, grammatically correct sentences, expressing millions of thoughts and experiences and observations can be formed. Sentences have 'emergent' qualities that the letters and spaces composing them do not possess. They can be gentle or inflammatory. Unlike individual letters, they can communicate information, persuade, mislead, enable actions or start a riot. In an analogous way, Lucretius suggested, starting with combinations of 'primitive' elements with only a few properties, everything in the noisy, colourful world of experience can be produced.

When it came to vision and hearing, the ancient Epicureans held the interesting theory that sights and sounds were rather like scents. 'Various sounds,' says Lucretius, 'are continually floating through the air ... When we walk near the sea, a briny taste often makes its way into our mouth; ... From all objects emanations flow away and are discharged in all directions on every side.' When we smell bacon frying in another room or catch a whiff of someone's perfume, we can infer that tiny particles made up of still smaller atoms have drifted into our noses from some distance. Tiny particles flow into our eyes and ears as well. For the Epicureans, when I see a tree, a thin 'film' of coloured particles actually detaches itself from the tree and floats into my eyes. Objects, they supposed, were constantly emitting these films from their surfaces and so wearing away, while replenishing their substance by absorbing particles from the environment.

Lucretius noted how dependent colours were on the conditions of observation and the lighting. This was especially noticeable in the case of the sea, whose colour varies from hour to hour. Colour, he inferred, must depend on the arrangement of atoms in physical objects and liquids, and how it is affected by light and affects our eyes. The same must be true for scents and tastes: the particles of what we smell and savour enter our bodies and are perceived as pleasant or unpleasant, as the case may be. He pointed out that physical processes such as grinding could change a dark substance like horn to a white powder. He drew from this a correct conclusion: objects do not have fixed, permanent colours, though colours appear to be relatively stable. The tomatoes on my countertop, for example, tend to look the same uniform shade of red to me whenever I see them, regardless of the lighting. Artists, however, are trained to notice the subtle differences that depend on illumination.

Today, no one who has actually studied the visual system believes that vision occurs via films peeling off the surface of objects and travelling through the air. Nor do we believe that the entities that will survive the collapse of our universe will be anything like a dust mote, only smaller. Nevertheless, Epicurean physics is the ancestor of our modern physics, and the developing notion of the atom can be traced from its first appearance in ancient Indian and Greek philosophy. Chemistry employs the notion of an atom of a chemical element such as carbon, gold or uranium, and light is often described as a stream of particles, the photons. But we now recognise that the chemical atom is itself a composite of subatomic particles, and that it can be split, liberating vast quantities of energy – a concept the Epicureans did not recognise.

According to Epicurean cosmology, nothing that we are aware of and experience can be considered permanent. Where the universe that we probe with radio telescopes and other devices is concerned, it will probably last for a few more billion years before returning to its elements, or mutating into some new form altogether. We cannot, however, rule it out that some singularity, unpredictable by our current physics, should bring about the total collapse of our universe two minutes from now. Once all of life disappears from the universe, it may never return. Or universes may cycle in and out of existence, reinventing time, space and matter, and bringing forth new and wondrous forms, even intelligent beings.

In the meantime, everything we see, touch and know about not only can be, but will be reduced to its unknown constituents. 'Time,' Lucretius says, 'wholly destroys the things it wastes and sweeps away, and engulfs all their substance.' Nothing in nature or made by us endures. This applies to our clothes and furnishings, which wear out, to our bodies that weaken and sag and are eventually reduced to dust. It applies to empires, to economic systems and to our relationships with friends and relatives, even to those that are only brought to an end by death.

As long as our world remains intact, however, new things come into existence as the elements move, interact and combine. New life replaces the old with the birth of children and grandchildren: 'Venus escort[s] each kind of creature back into the light of life.' We build new houses in new styles, sew new garments and invent new musical, artistic and political forms. We accept and sometimes welcome the changes in our relationships and the formation of new ones. 'No visible object ever suffers total destruction,' Lucretius points out, 'since nature renews one thing from another, and does not sanction the birth of anything unless she receives the compensation of another's death.'

ATOMISM: THREE CONSEQUENCES

The Epicureans drew several important consequences from their views about the nature of reality. The world of familiar objects – tables, chairs, plants and animals, puddles and ponds – its colours, scents and sounds, they realised, is an appearance. And although everything except the atom is perishable, some things are more stable and can endure longer than others. Organisms and boulders are stable by comparison with soap bubbles or houses of cards.

Taking this perspective on board, we realise that the perception of what we call reality depends on the observer, who is nothing but an aggregate of atoms (or their modern equivalent). Human beings are similar enough in our constitutions that we can all perceive tables and chairs, plants and animals, airplanes overhead, sails in the distance, red and green traffic lights, when they are a suitable distance away and our eyes are working normally. And human bodies are different enough from one another that we disagree about what dishes, colour combinations and perfumes are appealing. But the visual world of an eagle or a panther, the odiferous world of a dog, or that of a lizard that can smell carrion several miles away, must be different from ours, insofar as their bodies and sensory organs are composed of differently put-together particles. We should beware of supposing that human perception sets any kind of standard, as though other animals enjoy enhanced or suffer from defective versions of our perceptual abilities.

Individual differences can be strongly marked when it comes to the *values* – positive or negative – we 'see' in objects, situations and events, or feel 'belong' to them. We believe that strawberries are truly red and truly delicious when ripe, and that premeditated murder for financial gain is truly wrong. But we can only make such confident judgements because certain arrangements of particles, those composing strawberries or making up the pixels on a television screen at a certain time or the print in a newspaper article, make more or less the same impact on different human sensory systems and minds.

When we disagree in our perceptions or our moral judgements, the reason for this is not hard to fathom. We are similar but not identical, and the world presents itself a little differently to everyone. Please don't jump to the conclusion, however, that an Epicurean must be a relativist who thinks everyone's judgement is as good as everyone else's when it comes to questions of taste or morality. The actual Epicurean position on the issue of relativism is far subtler.

To return to the theme of atomic reality, the realisation that everything is fragile and tends with time to get broken up points us in two directions. First, we should not be surprised that our wine glasses break, our houses crumble, stock market runs come to an end and our relationships go awry. Forewarned is fore-armed. At the same time, we can appreciate that some objects and situations are more likely to hold up over time, either because, like boulders, they are large, hard and resistant, or because, like the soft human body and like some relationships, they can repair themselves 'from within'.

The Epicurean recognises that the tendency to fall apart is built into the nature of things. Aware that this is so, she preserves, repairs and restores where this is in her power, and accepts the inevitable when it is not. Further, she recognises that the future is genuinely open and unpredictable. We do not know what combinations will come along or what accidental 'swerves' will upset a delicate balance and make for sudden reversals. The Epicurean expects the future to be predictable and stable where experience and science have shown it to be so, but she is always prepared for surprises.

2

HOW DID WE GET HERE?

*From time everlasting countless elements of things,
impelled by blows and by their own weight, have
never ceased to move in manifold ways, making all kinds
of unions, and experimenting with everything they could
combine to create.*

Lucretius

*Many species of animals must have perished and failed to
propagate and perpetuate their race. For every species that
you see breathing the breath of life has been protected
and preserved from the beginning of its existence either
by cunning or by courage or by speed.*

Lucretius

The Epicurean believes that there was always something. There was never a time when nothing existed. This something was not, we now know, matter, but the precursor of matter. Today, we are told of fluctuations in the quantum vacuum of virtual particles, flickering in and out of existence, that gave birth to space, time and matter. Explosive events studded space with stars in which the elements of the periodic table were born, and the world we experience now emerged from a disorganised state of matter in motion that fell into stable configurations over perhaps 14 billion years. Our earth was a molten mass spun off from the sun whose geological features – its continents, oceans and mountains – were formed by violent physical processes as it cooled down.

In the ancient seas, some hundreds of millions of years after the formation of planet earth about 4.5 billion years ago, bombardment by lightning is thought to have produced organic molecules, including amino acids, which are composed of carbon, nitrogen, hydrogen and oxygen and which are the building blocks of proteins. These were stable molecules that came together to form protein strands that were also relatively stable and served as templates that formed other molecules into identical strands. Structures that held together and copied themselves proliferated, and varied, adding small increments of complexity and joining up with others. The others just fell apart.

Or perhaps these stable organic molecules were formed somewhere else in the universe and seeded our earth, arriving in meteors or in the icy tails of comets. In either case, the first single-celled organisms emerged around 3.85 billion years ago. Some were able to join up with others to form larger stable complexes. The 'struggle for existence' has accordingly been happening for nearly 4 billion years. Time, chance and the operation of the forces described by physics and chemistry have been sufficient to produce everything we see around us.

THE EPICUREAN THEORY OF NATURAL SELECTION

Many of us were taught in school, or at least came away with the impression, that until Charles Darwin published his *On the Origin of Species* in 1859, 'everybody' believed that the world had been created by a divinity in seven days, that Adam and Eve were the first human beings, and that Noah's Ark housed all the originally created animals. This is incorrect. Although Christianity and Judaism share this account, and although the Islamic account is similar to it, the other major religions, such as Buddhism, Hinduism and Confucianism, have their own accounts, and stories about how the world came to be are found in every culture on earth.

Further, the ancient Greek philosophers who preceded the Epicureans imagined the origins of the universe and its inhabitants in very different ways, as arising, for example, from the interactions of Love and Strife. Intriguingly, the ancient Epicureans themselves grasped the basic principle of what Darwin later called 'natural selection', anticipating some elements of his theory of evolution without having any real notion of the time scales involved and without understanding how one species could possibly give rise to another.

The Epicureans proposed that combinations of atoms taking the form of animals developed by chance or from atomic 'seeds' buried in the earth. Animals with features that favoured their survival, such as cunning, courage and speed, were able to persist longer than others that lacked these features. Over time, animals whose internal structure happened to create copy-creating copies of themselves arose by chance. If nature hadn't stumbled on such devices in the distant past, we wouldn't be around to observe other living things and to have thoughts about the origins of life. 'I am anxious that you should carefully avoid the mistake,' Lucretius says, 'of supposing that the lustrous eyes were created to enable us to see; or that the tapering shins and thighs were attached to the feet as a base to enable us to walk.' All such explanations, he adds, 'are propounded preposterously with topsy-turvy reasoning ... Sight did not exist before the birth of the eyes.'

This position was long ridiculed as absurd. The 'random concourse of atoms', it was alleged, could never have produced functioning living bodies and the regular movements of the heavenly bodies. But thanks to its perceived absurdity, it remained a target of criticism and stayed fresh in the minds of philosophers.

It is not so difficult to believe that the geological features of the earth appeared on account of the laws of physics and chemistry, that no intelligent being had to design them and make them. But life, in its complexity and diversity, has always posed much more of an explanatory problem. How could roses, peacocks and tigers, not to mention human beings, have come into the world through the operation of the laws of physics and chemistry? How could not only structure, but behaviour, such as the ability to build hives composed of hexagonal cells, as bees do, or the ability to use the stars for orientation in migration, as birds do, have arisen from the unguided motion of atoms in the void? These animals seem to have been intentionally fashioned to be beautiful and adorn the world, or to be good hunters or flyers, or producers of useful foodstuffs for us.

The creative action of God was compared in the Jewish, Christian and Islamic traditions to the activity of fashioning a figure or a pot from clay; references to the 'hand' or 'hands' and 'finger' of God are frequent in our literature. As the ancient painter took over where the ancient potter left off, and decorated the pot with the figures of birds, animals and humans, so God was thought of as making and embellishing the world. The theory of divine creation became more rather than less plausible in the period of the 17th-century Scientific Revolution when the intricacies of the bodies of insects and the tissues of other animals were first revealed by the microscope and when the 'mechanics' of the human body, considered to be a kind of hydraulic system working by the pressure of blood, lymph and cerebrospinal fluids in its vessels, began to be worked out. An argument widely considered irrefutable, and frequently presented in the 18th century, went more or less as follows: if I were to find a watch lying in the sand on a beach, I would never suppose that it had come into existence just by chance, or thanks to the laws of physics. And I would not expect a watch to produce little watches. Obviously, such a contrivance had to have been made by an intelligent being that had a purpose in mind, namely telling the time.

The same thought would have occurred to anyone in the early 19th century who stumbled on a woollen mill in a clearing in the woods, or anyone in the 20th century who encountered an automobile factory that turned sheets of steel and other materials into functional cars. Watches, mills and factories have to be carefully thought out and put together by a group of intelligent and capable beings – or by one extremely intelligent and extremely capable being – to succeed in doing what they do.

Animals somewhat resemble watches, mills and factories. Like watches, they have a lot of small moving parts. Like mills and factories, they transform inert basic materials – air, food and water – into functioning tissues and organs. Their individual parts work together in an integrated, harmonious manner to make life and reproduction possible, as the springs and wheels of the watch or the various components of the mill or factory function to turn the hands on the dial or deliver blankets, shawls and cars. The conclusion that animals – the first prototypes, at least – had been designed and created by a supernatural being looked inescapable.

The ancient Epicureans were not impressed by the argument that integration and harmony always imply a mastermind creator or a team working closely together with oversight of the whole process of manufacture. But as watches and automobile factories were in their time unknown, no one was around to present to them the argument that such complex and well-functioning things can't make themselves or appear by chance. If they had been confronted with such arguments, they *might* have insisted that a watch or a factory could arise through the chance combination of atoms. But I suspect they would have had to agree that it is probably impossible for a watch or a factory to assemble by chance. For this to happen, the various components would have to stick together and start to interact in just the right way. And to imagine a fly or a mouse or an elephant coming to be in this way strains credulity too far. Isn't this like expecting (as 20th-century critics of evolutionary theory used to argue) monkeys with typewriters to produce the plays of Shakespeare?

This was a stumbling block that seemed to give the advantage to Creationism.

I can well understand that a person brought up on the Genesis story of the creation of the universe in seven days and sitting in the classroom listening to a lecture on how Darwin discovered the theory of evolution by natural selection would be sceptical about his supposed achievement. Such a person might reasonably wonder: how could just one scientist in the 19th century looking at finch beaks in the Galapagos, and talking to pigeon breeders in England, prove that we evolved over hundreds of millions of years from apes and monkeys, which in turn evolved from something like fish and worms?

Even if you favour the Darwinian view over the Genesis story, it is good to remember that, on the face of it, it is somewhat implausible. But conversely, if you find Darwinism implausible, it is helpful to stop thinking of Darwin as suddenly and single-handedly coming up with a new and startling theory for which there is still no conclusive evidence. You can think of him instead as one of a long line of thinkers familiar with Epicurean philosophy who found the way over its major stumbling blocks where the theory of natural selection was concerned.

DARWIN'S UPGRADE:
HOW SELECTION CAUSES EVOLUTION

Lucretius's claim that nature had experimented with unsuccessful animal species that lacked the right structure to maintain themselves and reproduce was well known to the 18th- and early-19th-century theorists with whom Darwin was familiar. (One of them was his own grandfather, Erasmus Darwin, the author of a long poem on the origins and evolution of life). The early, hostile reviews of *On the Origin of Species* all mentioned its relationship with the Lucretian text. One reviewer complained, for example, that there was nothing new in Darwin's 'speculative' cosmogony. 'It is at least as old,' he said, 'as Democritus and Epicurus, and has never been presented with more poetic beauty than by Lucretius.'

Darwin did not attach his own account to Epicureanism, and especially to Lucretius's version, for obvious reasons. First, Lucretius (and grandfather Darwin) were notorious atheists, and Darwin kept or tried to keep his sceptical views on religion to himself. Second, he had to fend off the charge that his theory of evolution was a poetic fantasy or mere speculation. What, then, was he able to add to (and subtract from) the Epicurean theory that plants and animals evolved 'by chance' that changed its status in his mind and eventually in the minds of his early followers? How did Darwinism go beyond speculation to develop into an accepted account of the origin of the various species?

By the time the 19th century rolled around, most naturalists were doubtful that the astonishing number of different species then identified – far too many to have fitted on the Ark – including hundreds of different species of beetles, had been created by twos and on purpose. The true age of the earth had been calculated, and the former existence of the dinosaurs and the giant mammals that had once roamed Europe and Asia was generally known. Two scientific developments transformed the Epicurean theory of the natural origins of plants and animals from a somewhat implausible speculation to a well-founded scientific hypothesis. These were: the cell theory, and the notion of 'variation' from generation to generation.

The discovery, based on the microscope, unavailable to ancient philosophers, that all plants and animals were combinations of individual living cells, and that some cells were free-living animals like the amoeba, made it possible to think of the origins of life in terms of the first appearance of a living cell. To imagine, as Epicureanism required, an elephant emerging from a combination of atoms or even from an atomic seed in the earth was far more difficult than imagining a few single cells forming by chance and later joining up into larger cellular units.

Another obstacle for the Epicurean theory was the assumption that animals always gave birth to animals like themselves. This seemed obvious to them. Cows did not give birth to sheep, or blackbirds to swallows. This meant that they had to stick to their theory that the original prototypes of every sort of animal had sprung by chance from the earth. Although they fancied that not all of these animal types had been capable of survival and reproduction, they could not envision the descent of one kind of bird or mammal from an entirely different kind of bird or mammal.

Darwin's breakthrough occurred when he reflected on the selective breeding farmers had carried on for millennia, choosing from the pack or flock or herd, and breeding together male and female dogs, sheep and cattle with desired characteristics. He knew that within the group, individuals varied in their qualities and that offspring were not exactly like their parents. To the idea of *variation*, he was able to apply the Epicurean idea of *selection* – success or failure in living and reproducing.

For Darwin, nature, acting unconsciously, rather than the breeder acting with intention, did the selecting when the resources needed for life were limited and predation was the rule. Animals ate and sometimes killed plants and killed and ate one another. Bacteria, fungi and poisonous plants killed animals. Plants derived nutrition from decomposing animals. Naturalists had long wondered why, if the world was created by a supremely benevolent and skilled craftsman, this was how things worked. They also wondered why trees produced so many useless seeds and short-lived seedlings; why humans produced such an over-supply of 'spermatic animals'; and why so many children died in infancy. The grim truth was that competition for life was intense. Many individuals of a given species would starve, be eaten or die of accidents before reproducing, or fail to find or attract mates. Darwin argued that the appearance of entirely new species was the result of thousands or millions of generations of variation and selection in changing environments. The temporary stability that the Epicureans had ascribed to the world, which they saw as constantly evolving as the atoms fell into new combinations, was a feature of the individual species as well, and the mortality of the individual person applied to the whole species, whose eventual extinction was similarly inevitable.

Darwin's contribution, to my mind, was not just to think out how natural selection might work, but to show that it could be considered a *lawful* process rather than one based entirely on chance. For the constantly repeated accusation against the ancient Epicureans was that the beauty, intricacy and function-ality of the many forms of life could not arise from the random motions of atoms. But, in Darwin's view, the breeder who seeks

39

to improve his or her flock of sheep or hunting dogs, or the pigeon fancier who presents his or her fluffy tailed or brightly feathered specimens to other fanciers, is employing a technology, and wherever a technology is successful, there we expect to find laws of nature. Nature, too, must be employing a technology to create the succession of living forms of the past near 4 billion years.

To be sure, nature is not aiming to improve any individual species or the livestock or biomass of the planet itself. She is not trying to make animals or entire species faster, smarter or more beautiful. In fact, nature is not trying to do anything. But she mercilessly eliminates some members of each species who aren't keeping up with the others in producing, and in some cases raising to maturity, offspring who will have their own offspring. As a result, the face of living nature changes in ways we can often explain. Species have appeared and disappeared over the eons, and for this to have happened, there must be laws of nature underlying these changes. Chance – or what we think of as chance, namely coincidence – nevertheless plays a role. Many organisms perish, not because they lack strength, speed, cunning or good metabolisms, but just because they were in the wrong place at the wrong time. A good example is the class of dinosaurs that just happened to be inhabiting the earth 65 million years ago when it was hit 'by chance' – though fully in accord with the laws of physics – by an asteroid that wiped them all out.

The Lucretian account of the formation of the cosmos and the evolution of animals, and the Judaeo-Christian account of the divine creation of the world, were recognised as rivals from the early medieval period onwards. Their combat has been long and persistent, but also somewhat hidden from view, which is why Darwin receives too much credit for thinking out the basic idea of evolution by natural selection and too little credit for realising that variation was the key that could solve the problem of the origin of new species. The rivalry was not for a long time manifested in open debate because of the severe criminal penalties attached to blasphemy, a capital crime in earlier periods of Judaism, Christianity and Islam, and because of the ubiquity of censorship in many parts of Europe.

Why were ideas about the origins of life so dangerous? It was thought that if too many people began to take seriously accounts of the natural origins of life, they would cease to believe that they were created by and responsible to the God who had created them. If they stopped believing they were responsible to God, they would stop believing that obedience to God's commands and their rulers was obligatory and that disobedience would be harshly punished. If they stopped believing that obedience was obligatory, they would become libertines, criminals and revolutionaries.

Today, the fear that motivated execution for heretics and resulted in the banning, confiscation and burning of scientific books takes a different form. It is not fear of revolutionary violence that explains the persistence of Creationism and intelligent design theories. Some Creationists would probably like to overthrow their secular governments by force of arms and replace them with theocracies. The fear is rather that if the Epicurean–Darwinian theory is true and intelligent design false, divinities and religious texts are not sources of moral authority, and eternal life is not the reward for faith. In that case, there is no reason to obey the Ten Commandments or all the moral ordinances of one's own church. Moral anarchy, by which Creationists usually understand homosexuality, adultery, abortion and divorce, and the breakdown of the family and society, will result.

If the divine-command theory of morality were the only option, and if the inescapability of death actually spoiled our lives, worries about the social and psychological effects of accepting evolutionary theory might be justified. But it was Darwin himself, drawing on a long tradition of secular British moral theory as well as his own observations of birds and mammals, who first argued that certain forms of altruism characterised group living animals, contributing to their survival. Conscience, or a moral sense, would inevitably arise, he declared, in any social animal that had developed intelligence comparable to that of a human being.

More recent research on primates and young children has confirmed that the moral sentiment of empathy and the disposition to help others, along with a preference for fairness, are to some extent prefigured in our evolutionary ancestors and wired into us from birth. These endowments can be strengthened and extended, as Darwin saw, through formal learning, or weakened by experience and indoctrination. And despite having no conception whatsoever of the descent of one species from an entirely different one, the ancient Epicureans had a serviceable theory of natural morality that I'll explore in Chapter 6 (pages 95–108). They showed how it was possible to live cheerfully and ethically as a mortal.

3

THE MATERIAL MIND

The spirit ... is born with the body, develops with it, and succumbs with it to the stress and strain of age.

Lucretius

Even if you are not tempted by Creationism, you may well wonder how conscious awareness and the power of perception and thought – mind or spirit – could arise from combinations of material particles. In keeping with their sparse ontology of atoms and void, the ancient Epicureans declared the soul – the principle of movement, sensation, experience and thought in living beings – to be composed of a special sort of atom. 'Soul atoms', they proposed, were especially small, especially mobile and very lively. They pervaded the limbs of the human body, enabling us to think, feel and move. Unlike the soul of Christian and other theologies, the Epicurean soul was not immortal or an object of special care and concern by contrast with the body.

We feel and know that we are wholly united with our bodies, says Lucretius. 'The spirit's interpenetration of the body through veins, flesh, sinews and bones is so complete that even the teeth are given a share in sensation, as is shown by toothache, or the twinge caused by icy water, or the crunching of rough grit concealed in a piece of bread.' Too much wine has the effect of 'confounding the spirit within the body'. Now, 'the limbs become heavy; [the drunkards] reel about with staggering steps;

45

the tongue drawls, the mind is sodden, the eyes swim'. In an epileptic fit 'the spirit in every part of their frame is so distracted by the violence of the seizure that it surges and foams, just as the waves of the salt sea seethe beneath the furious force of the winds'.

Because body and mind are entirely interwoven, the body cannot live on and experience sensation without its mind, and the mind divorced from the body cannot produce any thought or movement. At the moment of death, the soul particles escape into the surrounding atmosphere without causing any immediate change in the weight or shape of the body. 'It is like the case of a wine whose bouquet has evaporated, or of a perfume whose exquisite scent has dispersed into the air, or of some object whose flavour has departed.' The death of the body most certainly means the permanent annihilation of that body's mind.

THE MYSTERY OF CONSCIOUSNESS

The 17th-century philosopher René Descartes, who had no problem with the Epicurean account of the origins of plants and nonhuman animals, famously balked at taking the same view of humans. Where plants and animals are just unconscious material machines, human beings, he argued, are material machines that also possess an incorporeal, immortal soul that endows them with conscious awareness, free will and rationality. Each human soul must have a divine origin. Not only did this claim excuse him from having to try to explain consciousness, free will and rationality in mechanical terms, it enabled the rest of his basically Epicurean 'corpuscularian' philosophy to make it past some of, though not all, the censors. (Despite his extensive references to God and the incorporeal soul, his books were viewed with considerable suspicion and for a time appeared on the Index of Prohibited Books of the Catholic Church.)

Descartes's official theory of the special human soul put him in good and extensive company. The majority of the human race believed in his time, and the majority still believes, that the soul is a *something* that lives in the body. The soul is thought of as a permanent, indestructible entity that can survive the death of the body. Not only can it survive, it can reattach itself to a new living body – either the resurrected body of the person who died, or one of their descendants, or an animal of another species – where it will continue to see, feel and think to the extent permitted by that body. The Epicurean of today will, however, insist that the soul is not able to detach itself from its original body or attach itself to another unensouled human body. My death, she supposes, will be the end of all *my* experience and thinking, and it will not be the start of some other being's experience and thinking, except in the sense that some of the particles composing me may eventually find their way into another organism.

But if we don't have immaterial and potentially immortal souls or minds, how can thought, experience and voluntary movement be explained? No one today can take seriously the idea of soul atoms. As we see it, there is something about how my living body is put together from individually lifeless and thoughtless particles that enables me to be conscious, aware of my environment, subject to pain, able to initiate actions, to reflect on myself and the world, to make plans and decisions, and to build and create. Nothing more than a brain, composed of molecules, which are composed of atoms, which are composed of subatomic particles, located in an animal body is needed for experience, thought and voluntary movement. And it is not a foregone conclusion that a brain is *necessary* for feeling and deciding. Other biological structures found in living beings, or even other structures or programs that could be placed into computers, might make thought and feeling possible.

The Evolution of Consciousness

It is currently thought that consciousness may be widely distributed in nature. There is little doubt that mammals and birds have experiences and feel emotions, and the sensation of pain must have appeared very early in evolutionary history. As difficult as it is to imagine the experiences of a gecko or a spider, many animals, including fish, reptiles, cephalopods like octopi and squid, and even insects, have a good claim to awareness of a sensory world of flavours, odours, sounds and visible, tangible objects and substances.

Still, it might seem incredible that consciousness and all our mental powers, including rational decision-making and creativity as well as perception and feeling, could arise from purely physical underpinnings, from processes in our brains that work according to the laws of physics and chemistry. The alphabet analogy goes some way towards explaining how individual elements – letters – can give rise to composites – words and sentences – with new qualities. But we may still wonder how, from the ultimately real colourless, odourless, tasteless, silent particles and forces, consciousness can present to us a world of flavour, colour, scent and sound.

No one has ever explained, scientifically, how we can be aware of a world and why we experience the qualities we do – why the scent of roses is as it is, and why certain wavelengths of light are correlated with the experience of red rather than the experience of blue. No one has ever explained how I can initiate an action voluntarily and deliberately. Nevertheless, the

Epicurean of today asks: which is more likely? That whether we can ever explain it or not, consciousness and mentality arise from purely physical underpinnings, nothing more being required? Or that a non-physical entity lives in us somewhere and, when connected properly to a functioning physical brain, enables the possessor of that brain to think, feel, perceive and decide?

A more tractable question than 'How does conscious awareness arise?' is the question of *why* conscious awareness is useful. Developing lungs or wings enabled prehistoric animals to exploit particular features of their environment: to move from the sea onto the land where there were new things to eat, or from land into the air, where many predators could be avoided. But what does having awareness, consciousness of a world and, with it, knowledge of how my body is related to other bodies enable me to accomplish what I couldn't accomplish if I were a well-programmed unconscious machine? With robotics constantly improving and developing remarkable recognition and navigation skills, this question is highly actual.

To see why, despite technological advances, consciousness might be necessary for many living things, consider the simple robot known as the Roomba. The Roomba is a disk, about 16 inches in diameter, with two independently operating wheels, that gets plugged into the wall to charge. It then runs around your floor sweeping up crumbs and dust. According to its literature, it is able to 'change direction upon encountering obstacles, to detect dirty spots on the floor and to sense steep drops to keep it from falling down stairs'.

The Roomba does only one thing, but it does it reasonably well: it forages for dust and dirt. Successive generations of Roombas evolve, because consumers want and will pay for upgraded models with fewer problems and more capabilities. It is, however, not a machine that transforms raw materials into energy and work. It does not use the dust and dirt it collects to keep running. Because it can draw on an unlimited supply of electricity from the wall to recharge its batteries, it does not need to be self-sustaining. It is highly dependent on its owner for continuing operation, for it can get stuck under furniture and run out of charge.

Now imagine we want to build a robot that forages for food outdoors on variable terrain, rather than for dust and dirt on flat indoor surfaces, and that it will convert this food into the fuel that powers its movements. It now faces certain dangers, not only from sharp rocks and precipices in its environment, but also from heat, cold and rain that will destroy its electronic components. It must avoid consuming non-food substances. It must be efficient in expending its energy if it is to survive, because the amount of food it can find, consume and metabolise for power is limited. This robot is mortal. It can just wear out, like the Roomba, through friction and corrosion. But it can also 'die' if its energy needs exceed the amount of food it is able to find, consume and convert to power, or if it fails to detect a lethal danger. It may also be attacked and killed by another robot that can consume its body for fuel or replacement components, or by an irritated human being.

Using present technologies, this robot will have very complex software. It will need to perceive the difference between food and non-food that closely resembles food. It will need a memory to avoid wasting energy searching in places where no food was found recently, but some such places may become good sources of food in the future, and it will need to remember that. In order to know when to start foraging and when to stop, it will need sensors that monitor its energy needs. It will need a decision mechanism that can make critical choices, such as the choice to continue its food search even when its energy stores are so low that it may 'die', or to abandon the search to conserve energy and to wait for food to replenish itself in the environment.

Now let's imagine that the robot can reproduce. It will build copies of itself that accidentally vary slightly. Either it must build full-size copies of itself or smaller variant copies that will grow as they consume nourishment. If the former, it will expend large amounts of energy; if the latter, new software will be needed to direct growth. A robot that exists among other robots competing for the same food and shelter and competing to be a faster producer of little robots will have to be endowed with better competencies than theirs. If it is a sexually reproducing robot, it will also need to be able to identify potential 'mates', and to perform courtship behaviour that is successful in inducing the other robot to cooperate.

By now it should be clear that it may be impossible from an engineering point of view to pack all these competencies into an unconscious machine operating on chips that is only the size of a Roomba, or to pack them into a unit the size of a mouse using only Roomba-type materials and structures. However the mouse is doing all that a Roomba does, it isn't doing it with Roomba-type materials and structures, and it is probably conscious. The mouse's ability to have experiences, to see, to recognise places and things, to remember locations, to make decisions, to choose mates, to feel the emotion of fear that enables it to avoid cats and boots, and the emotion of love that moves it to care for its young while they are small will make it an efficient and competitive organism. If evolution can tap into the laws of nature that make consciousness possible, the mouse will not need the fancy electronics and tremendous bulk and complexity that a foraging and reproducing robot would need if built with unconscious technology.

When we look at a human brain, a soft, lobular structure roughly the consistency of oatmeal, it is impossible to imagine it producing experiences and ideas. The case bears no comparison with, for example, looking at the liver, another soft, lobular structure, and wondering how it can produce liver enzymes; *someone* can no doubt explain this. Yet we know that the patterned excitation of the three trillion neurons in the average brain gives rise to what the neuroscientist Antonio Damasio calls 'the feeling of what happens'. Perhaps this is accomplished through the classical mechanisms of physics and chemistry, but an emerging trend is to propose that evolution has tapped into quantum mechanics. If organisms can tap into the laws of hydrodynamics to swim and fly efficiently, and the laws of action and reaction to push off from the earth in locomotion; if they can use photons to see, and to organise their circadian rhythms, why should they not be able to tap into quantum mechanics to master some of the challenges of life?

We tend to think of consciousness as all or nothing. We suppose that either a conscious organism experiences the world just as I do or that it is just an insensate machine. But this must be wrong. There must be forms and degrees of consciousness that are only somewhat or hardly at all like mine, as well as forms that are very like mine. If the nervous system first evolved to co-ordinate movement, we can imagine that a side effect of having just a little bit of conscious awareness – perhaps for pain or scent – could give an early organism an advantage and that nature continued to add on as new ways of gathering information from the environment through light or sound or scent were invented and new perceptual and emotional motivations assisted with the tasks of living.

Philosophers and neuroscientists continue to debate whether consciousness is accidental or intrinsically useful, whether it extends to invertebrates like the bee or the oyster, and whether it is only present in animals with brains of a certain complexity. The Epicurean can only follow these debates with interest, never doubting that the mind is, at any rate, a natural thing whose existence is dependent on the smallest particles and subtlest forces of the physical world.

4

THE STORY OF HUMANITY

The human beings who lived on earth in those early days were far tougher than we are ... [T]hey were not easily affected by heat or cold or unaccustomed food, or any physical malady. During many lustres of the sun revolving through the sky, they lived random-roving lives like wild beasts ... What the sun and rains had given them, what the earth had spontaneously produced, were gifts rich enough to content their hearts.

Lucretius

Although they belonged to the highly developed civilisations of ancient Greece and Rome, the ancient Epicureans were fascinated by the recognition that human beings had not always lived in cities or practised farming, industry and commerce. They were aware that their ancestors had formerly lived in families and tribes with little political organisation. They understood that they had only later come together into federations, empowered kings and magistrates, and enacted laws and systems of punishment for offences and crimes. Relying on the manuscripts of Epicurus, as well as on the knowledge of his contemporaries about the distant past, Lucretius thought deeply about the origins of civilisation, and in the fifth book of *On the Nature of Things* he narrated the story of humanity, drawing important conclusions about technological progress, human happiness and political oppression that deserve our continued attention.

THE STATE OF NATURE AND THE RISE OF CIVILISATION

Lucretius describes the earliest phase of human life as dangerous but in many ways attractive. Adults lived as solitary foraging animals (presumably carrying or followed by their children). Many were 'caught by wild beasts and provided them with living food for their teeth to tear', while others died of their wounds 'as no one knew anything of medicine'. But, says Lucretius pointedly, 'Never in those times did a single day consign to destruction many thousands of men marching beneath military standards; never did the boisterous billows of the ocean dash ships and sailors upon the rocks.' People died of famine, but not of surfeit; they got poisoned accidentally from eating the wrong thing, whereas 'nowadays they make away with themselves more expertly'.

Fire was not stolen from the gods, as the Greek myth of Prometheus had it, nor was it a divine gift. Rather, Lucretius explains, forest fires were frequent in those early days, caused by lightning or the friction of tree branches rubbing against one another. People figured out how to capture, control and preserve fire, and this marked a turning point. They grew used to warmth and drew together to live as families in huts. They learned to cook their food, and living with women and children made men gentler and more obliging. Human language, which Lucretius saw as just another form of animal language, was invented, along with crafts such as plaiting and weaving. Although they fought with stones and clubs, early humans could not do each other much damage. There was relative equality and relative freedom without priests and judges to lay down the laws and threaten punishment.

Lucretius's reconstruction has been largely validated by archaeologists and students of the few remaining hunter-gatherer societies. Anthropologists have noted the 'preference for equality' in small and simple societies and the resentment of anyone who begins to act in an aggressive manner. There may be a headman in larger tribal societies, but his main function is to negotiate with outsiders, not to make rules for insiders, and he does not normally distinguish himself in dwelling or dress. How, then, did human beings make the transition from living in small, relatively egalitarian groups to oligarchies and imperial bureaucracies? In these political structures, wealth and power are concentrated in a small number of hands, and a very few rulers make decisions affecting the experiences and even the survival of millions of their subjects. For, as Lucretius emphasises, though he perhaps exaggerates the uninterrupted harmony of archaic life, warfare was unknown. All motivation to attack the neighbours was lacking, as well as effective weapons for doing so.

Lucretius is vague about how this happened. He supposes that 'those endowed with exceptional talents and mental power' invented new and admired practices and that kings appeared who rewarded their favourites and built cities. The invention of money brought in a new political era. 'Later, wealth was invented and gold discovered, [which] robbed the strong and handsome of their prestige; for as a general rule ... people ... follow in the train of the rich.'

In Lucretius's account, archaic society came to an end with a chance discovery, the discovery of the metals: copper, gold, iron, silver and lead. People observed how, in the immediate aftermath of a forest fire, metals oozed and ran out of rocks and solidified in new shapes. Here was a material that was far harder and more durable than wood and that, unlike stone, could be formed as one wished. Human ingenuity took over, and with metal technology came agricultural slavery, class divisions and brutal conquest. 'With bronze they tilled the soil, and with bronze they embroiled the billows of war, broadcast wide gaping wounds; and plundered flocks and fields; for everything unarmed and defenceless readily yielded to the armed.'

Contemporary archaeology bears out Lucretius's view that cities, trade and warfare evolved rapidly with the introduction of metal technology. With the plough and draft animals, human beings could now till vast fields and grow, store and trade grain, the new staple of the diet of the poor. With saws and hammers they could build houses, walls and fences to keep people indoors and livestock segregated. Carts for trade and travel could be furnished with wheels and drawn by domesticated animals. Tools applied to mining brought up precious metals and gems. With the new abundance of food wrested from the soil, populations grew and markets expanded. The art of shipbuilding made long-distance travel possible. A vast gap began to open up between rich and poor. The rich were those who persuaded or forced others to work for them in the fields, to manufacture tools and ornaments, to build dwellings for them and to fight their battles. The poor were those who had no choice but to enslave themselves to the rich.

This process involved gains and losses. Life became safer in some ways, and the countryside was beautified, 'attractively dotted with sweet fruit trees and enclosed with luxuriant plantations'. Village life remained idyllic, Lucretius thought. People would lie in the grass in friendly company and 'there would be jokes, talk and peals of pleasant laughter'. Bedecked with garlands of flowers, they amused one another with simple, rather clumsy dances. Singing was a good remedy for insomnia.

At the same time, everything got worse in other respects. Shipbuilding made long-distance warfare possible. Iron spears were far deadlier than Stone Age weapons, and there was now more to fight for. In the cities, the rich began to vie among themselves for wealth and power, and a period of bloodshed and chaos ensued. '[T]he situation sank to the lowest dregs of anarchy, with all seeking sovereignty and supremacy for themselves. At length some of them taught the others to create magistracies and established laws ... The reason why people were sick and tired of a life of violence was that each individual was prompted by anger to exact vengeance more cruelly than is now allowed by equitable laws.' If humans had not invented law and bureaucracy, that would have been an end to our species. But they did. Criminality was suppressed, enabling wealthy civilisations to advance further with the building of roads, the erection of palaces and the creation of artworks.

As we now know, ancient artisanship produced objects of utility and beauty for trade and domestic use, but only by making use of slave labour in huge urban workshops. The concentration of settled populations fostered learning in mathematics, astronomy, philosophy and other sciences, as well as the great feats of ancient engineering. It also produced a parasitic upper class that lived from the hard labour of others, enjoying their rents, tax revenues and inheritances, but at the same time gnawed by anxiety over managing and retaining their wealth. Whether rich or poor, Lucretius observed, 'human beings never cease to labour vainly and fruitlessly, consuming their lives in groundless cares, evidently because they have not learned the proper limit to possession, and the extent to which real pleasure can increase'. Ambition, aggression and corruption render societies that appear externally to be flourishing internally rotten.

AUTHORITY AND INEQUALITY

There are two especially important features of Epicurean prehistory. First, the Epicurean account invites us to reflect on the nature of power and political authority. Second, Lucretius's account of the gains and losses of civilisation will resonate with anyone concerned about the effects of technological progress and development on human well-being and the well-being of the rest of life on our planet.

Political authority, in the Epicurean view, does not belong to nature. It exists 'by convention'. That is to say, there are many forms of government, all of which depend on some form of human acquiescence, and what we define as criminal behaviour and what penalties we impose on lawbreakers are matters of human decision. Rules such as 'an eye for an eye' do not constitute natural justice; they rather reflect good or bad decisions about appropriate punishment. Penalties such as a certain number of years in prison for kidnapping, murder or fraud do not fit the crime in any objective sense. They have simply been deemed appropriate by lawmakers, sometimes for no good reason.

The significance of the Epicurean view was considerable. It challenged the prevailing assumption that authority and justice were defined in advance of human decisions and agreement. The Epicurean invites us to distinguish between *naked authority* – the raw exercise of *power*: the power to make laws, to establish rules for institutions, to inflict suffering on others, or to reward them with what they value – and *legitimate authority*, arising out of human agreement.

The original human interpretation of political authority was theological. In archaic and tribal societies, the gods were or are conceived as owning the land and its living beings. They, or subordinate spirits, are imagined to lay down laws concerning permitted and impermissible actions where the rest of nature and other people are concerned. In some tribal societies, divine ownership entailed judicious use of natural resources, especially game, along with other rules for living, strongly or weakly enforced.

In any case, theological accounts of political authority emphasise the power of the gods to punish actions that escape human notice. The Judaeo-Christian-Islamic Bible opens with an account of God's creative power and his legislative authority. It describes his instructions to the first human pair in his personally owned garden, their disobedience and the terrible consequences of their disobedience. The authority of God's first prophet Moses, who commands people to leave Egypt and form a new nation, is authority conferred upon him by God. And in Christian political theory, temporal rulers are theorised as placed and held in power by God and as owed a duty of obedience in light of their origin. For the religiously orthodox person, if God didn't want some particular person to be president of the United States, that person would not be president, so whatever that person does must be consistent with God's will.

A rival and equally influential tradition regarded political authority as built into the very structure of the universe. Epicurus's predecessor, the Greek philosopher Aristotle, thought it obvious that the cosmos is hierarchically organised. The superior, he said, always rules the inferior. The heavens rule the earth below them, causing the seasons, which cause weather, which determines the food supply and reproductive behaviour. Many animal species have dominant individuals; masters rule their slaves; men rule women; and women rule children. This is the natural order of things, he maintained, and it would be perverse to question it. His views on natural domination offered one regrettable interpretation of the ancient ideal of 'life in accord with nature'.

In the Middle Ages and in the early modern period, there could be tension and conflict between the Church's own wealthy hierarchy of the Pope, the archbishops, the bishops and the lesser clergy and the secular emperors, kings and princes. Both had the power to raise revenues and to make rules. No ordinary person, no peasant farmer, or merchant, or artisan, or small landowner could doubt that the power to command, punish and reward descended from above. The forms these commands, punishments and rewards took did not depend on the agreement of those affected, but only on the social class into which they were born. As a result, there were different legal standards for the privileged and the poor, for men and women, and for different categories of persons such as the hereditary nobility and the clergy. The relative invulnerability of the socially powerful permitted extraordinary abuses: the waging of private wars and raids to increase wealth and dominion; the execution of rivals and confiscation of their estates; favouritism towards the incompetent; and the sexual abuse of women and children.

In the medieval and early modern periods, it has been estimated that 80–90 per cent of the population of the Holy Roman Empire were peasants or renters, tied to the land, paying tithes, rents or taxes to their landlord and serving as soldiers when required. The clergy, the aristocracy and craftspersons made up the rest of the population. Indoctrination in the form of weekly sermons inculcated the duty of obedience. Revolution, a literal turning upside down of social relations, putting those at the bottom on top and those on top at the bottom, was seen as a crime against God and nature. The assurance that Heaven awaited those who endured their sufferings and deprivations and patiently practised humility was offered on a weekly basis. The sufferings and deprivations of the people were by implication trivial as compared to those of the great martyrs, including Jesus himself, as the iconography of the churches emphasised.

Did those at the bottom passively accept their subordination? Were their lives uniformly miserable? As historians have shown us, village life had its share of joys and sorrows. Yet history is dotted with slave revolts and peasant uprisings prompted by taxation demands and starvation. Most rebellions were successfully put down, yet massive changes occurred between the 17th and mid-19th centuries. The transformation of these feudal societies based on the privileges and duties of the different social ranks into commercial societies based on the idea of contracts between equals has been studied from many points of view. The recovery of the Epicurean history of humanity, the distinction between nature and convention, and the Epicurean conception of justice as an agreement to avoid harming and being harmed, played an important role in rethinking questions about the legitimacy and scope of worldly powers.

Up until the mid-17th century, when Thomas Hobbes appeared on the scene, the idea of natural domination as well as the idea of divine legislation went largely unquestioned. Hobbes's revival of the Epicurean idea of the 'social contract', which I'll explore in Chapter 12 (pages 205–23), though it is still authoritarian rather than democratic, is the basis of much modern political theory, with its clear insistence that government exists only for the good of the governed.

The Lessons of the Past

One of the most important insights to take away from Lucretian prehistory and its reworking is that the purpose of political authority is to reduce interpersonal violence and to make life secure for all. A second insight is that our political and legal systems have been shaped by chance discoveries and new technologies. A third is that while life under civilisation offers a range of marvellous goods and experiences, uncontrolled and concentrated wealth and ambition make exploitation, warfare and corruption inevitable.

There is no cosmic plan in history, no destiny towards which we are inevitably travelling. No divinity is guiding us or watching out that we do not make mistakes that unleash nuclear war or that render most other species extinct and the earth uninhabitable. Chance discoveries are still possible, and human ingenuity is seemingly inexhaustible. But the search for power and gratification by the few at the expense of the many is an inevitable feature of civilisation that could be better controlled than it is, even if it can never be banished once and for all.

Another important insight emerges from the Epicurean history of humanity. Human beings invented government. We like to think of government as authority awarded to those most deserving of it, to people who have proved their commitment to the general welfare and their understanding of how the world works by presenting their beliefs and plans to the public, and by standing up to interrogation in competition with others. But we need to keep in mind that modern governments are the successors of originally kleptocratic, clan-based regimes that relied on secrecy, conspiracy, violence and intimidation to obtain and retain power and wealth and to practise violence against other groups. To a greater or lesser extent, they have either retained or shed the earlier characteristics of government. The best governments are those that have transcended their origins, rejected the seizure of power by force and fraud, and are now dedicated not to the enrichment of the clan, but to the welfare and best interests of the governed. The worst governments are those in which most of the original features of government are intact.

PART II

LIVING WELL AND LIVING JUSTLY

5

ETHICS AND THE
CARE OF THE SELF

*The cry of the flesh: not to be hungry, not to be thirsty,
not to be cold. For if someone has these things and is
confident of having them in the future, he might
contend even with Zeus for happiness.*

Epicurus

*I ... do not even know what I should conceive the good to be,
if I eliminate the pleasures of taste, and eliminate the
pleasures of sex, and eliminate the pleasures of listening,
and eliminate the pleasant motions caused in our
vision by a sensible form.*

Epicurus

E thics is the study of how to live and what to do. As Epicurus says, it is about personal 'choice and avoidance'. It is about *my* decisions on what to pursue and what to avoid, and avoidance is as important as choice.

PLEASURE AND PAIN

The Epicurean believes that nature is the ultimate source of the 'oughts', 'mays', and 'may nots' that play an important role in human life. He regards sensory, emotional and intellectual pleasures as the goods worthy of being chosen – though ethics, as the following chapters will show, puts limits on these choices. He regards physical and psychological pain as the evils to be avoided and prevented. Nobody, Epicurus thought, has to command us to care for ourselves in this way. Nobody naturally seeks out situations of physical pain, anxiety and fear; nobody avoids situations that bring gratification, relief and release of tensions. That goes for so-called masochists as well. Masochists seek and obtain pleasure and release of tension by stimulating their fear and pain receptors.

If you think with Epicurus that pleasure is our 'first and only good', you are not in the company of the wise, at least not in the tradition of Western philosophy. The great philosophers have denigrated and warned against pleasure from time immemorial. For instance:

Plato: 'Pleasure is the greatest incentive to evil.'
Aristotle: 'Most pleasures are bad.'
Epictetus: 'It is the nature of the wise to resist pleasure.'
Kant: 'Whoever wants to be quite happy must remain
   indifferent towards pain and pleasure.'

To be fair, these quotes are taken out of context, and in at least some of these writers, you will find defences of pleasure suitably qualified. For example, the pleasures of heaven may be deemed desirable, and the pursuit of moral virtue may be deemed to give rise to an acceptable form of pleasure. But sensory pleasure and especially sexual pleasure are typically hedged with warnings from moral philosophers and theologians. That, one often feels, is their *job*. Philosophers may agree that animals in general pursue pleasure, but the point is often made that human beings are superior to other animals in being able to repress their desires. From this it is thought to follow that they should practise their superiority by doing so. Ascetic routines such as fasting, being cold and wearing uncomfortable garments are associated in many cultures with holiness and a status above that of the ordinary person.

What are the arguments against pleasure? They are rarely stated explicitly, indicating perhaps that many humans have a deeply rooted ambivalence to pleasure that needs only to be refreshed from time to time by philosophical and religious reminders. We all seem to know intuitively that pleasure and danger are associated, and that sexual pleasure is the most dangerous of all pleasures, far exceeding in this regard the dangers of overindulgence in food, or drink, or too much enjoyment of art, music, dance and travel. In fact, these other activities are sometimes tainted by the association of other pleasures with sexual pleasure. Even Epicurean theory comes with its own set of warnings about pleasure.

PRUDENCE AND ITS LIMITS

To the question 'Should we all do what we feel most like doing at any given moment, since our liking for pleasure and our aversion to pain are natural and fundamental?' the Epicurean answer is, 'Absolutely Not.' To explain this answer, I'll discuss first what philosophers term self-regarding actions, i.e., actions that have little or no effect on anyone else but a noticeable effect on the self. The next chapter will discuss 'other-regarding' actions from an Epicurean perspective.

Where self-regarding actions are concerned, Epicurus reminds us that the pursuit of small pleasures now can bring on severe pains later, while the endurance of certain pains now can bring on more pleasures down the road. I need to choose and avoid *prudentially*, in view of the long-term effects of actions that are readily foreseeable. It is sensible to undergo the mild pain of having one's teeth scraped to prevent the major troubles of having them rot and fall out later and to get the prick of a vaccination to escape a disabling disease. More painful and tiring medical interventions may be justified by their positive impact on functioning once the wounds have healed. Limiting vacation expenses now to ensure a comfortable old age and reducing the consumption of delicious pastries to prevent diabetes in middle age is, according to the Epicurean, rational forward-thinking self-care. Refusing to think about longer-term consequences may be pleasant now, but the long-term consequences of failing to think about those consequences can be very painful.

At the same time, it is possible to be *too oriented* towards the future. A hangover may be a fair price to pay for a really fantastic evening, even if a decline into the horrors of addiction is too high a price to pay for a long series of really fantastic evenings. Our ability to predict the future is limited, and a good and happy life can accommodate some risk. Many commercial interests are involved in selling us prudential goods, including examinations, operations and insurance policies that we don't need but that we are readily persuaded – by the arousing of psychologically unpleasant fear and anxiety – that we do need. For example, my local water company once offered to sell homeowners insurance against one of their supply pipes under the road breaking and flooding their houses. This would be an enormous nuisance if it happened, my imagination assures me, and it would be nice to have a pay-out from the water company to get my house dried out and repaired. But maybe the risk is low enough that my money is better directed elsewhere.

The question 'How prudent should I be in this case?' is one that the Epicurean of today thinks should always be investigated empirically, even if the decision, in the end, depends on your preferences. Given the statistics, you may decide that you do not really need water-pipe insurance or an extended warranty on your new dishwasher, or really stand to benefit from that mammogram. But what if you derive enormous comfort and security from warranties and tests? If, after you have acquainted yourself with the facts, insofar as they are known, about the likelihood of various outcomes, your fears and anxieties can only be relieved by the tests and warranties, the Epicurean would advise you to disburden yourself of these pains. Conversely, if you have really familiarised yourself with the medical literature on, say, smoking, and are well informed about its effects on heart, lungs, skin, circulatory system, teeth and so on, but you just love to smoke, then, in conditions where no one else is bothered by your smoke, and if no one will be harmed by your likely premature advance to decrepitude and death or by following your example, the Epicurean advice is: 'Go right ahead.'

Although the Epicurean favours just this kind of sensible, balanced approach, he or she is, technically, a *hedonist*. And it is not only stern old philosophers who customarily think of hedonism as essentially frivolous and as usurping the place of worthwhile, though not so pleasant, pursuits.

HEDONISM AND ITS PROBLEMS

The hedonist, we think, goes in for bubble baths, champagne brunches and massages. Advertising urges female consumers to 'treat yourself', by which they mean: eat some 'sinful' or 'decadent' sweets and purchase some custom vitamin packs and infrared sauna sessions. An article in *Cosmopolitan* magazine on how to treat yourself advises you to: consume chocolate, go shopping for a lipstick or 'glittery socks', stay home from work 'for no reason', purchase some 'yoghurt body wash' and wash your feet with it; moisturise your body with 'apricot and honey' body moisturiser, and make some mashed avocado and chilli toast to eat in bed. Male hedonism, as portrayed by advertisers and article writers in thrall to them, takes on a different face. It is associated with travel to tropical resorts, and with the purchase of expensive watches, belts, rings and bracelets, with driving performance cars, drinking whisky, and with non-committed, on-demand sex. There may be no serious long-term pains associated with these activities, but all this hardly sounds like ethical advice. Rather, it sounds like naked consumerism and avoidance of mental effort.

The authentic Epicurean looks at this advice with mixed feelings. The pleasures to be found in escaping the hustle and bustle of everyday life in sex, food, drink and comfortable surroundings are undeniable. But the purchase of smart accessories would not have crossed Epicurus's or Lucretius's mind as particularly pleasurable, and there are some further peculiarities in these visions of the alleged good life.

First, female hedonism in these presentations is associated with retreat to a safe space at home in bed and with low-budget self-pampering and grooming; male hedonism is associated with far-away adventures and high-budget conspicuous display. These differences tell us quite a bit about our society, about which gender controls most of the money, which gender is more likely to be enjoying their work and which attributes – smooth feet or fancy chronometers – are thought to be attractive to potential mates. The hedonists portrayed by advertisers are either shirking responsibility – staying home from work 'for no reason' – or have so much autonomy that they are free to take off for the tropics at any time.

Our advertisers understand well how all five senses can be engaged by the right products. But it is dismaying to think that to have the most enjoyable experiences the money at hand could buy, we need to curl up in bed or take a far-off vacation and enter a fantasy world of white sand beaches and palm trees. Vacations can be wonderful and memorable, but it is even better to integrate certain Epicurean values into the day-to-day world of work and family life.

The Epicurean won't give you a list of things to do to enjoy yourself, but she can remind you of the riches of the sensory world and encourage you to enjoy yourself. Unlike the majority of philosophers, past and present, she gives you permission to be an unapologetic sensualist, exercising avoidance as well as choice. By way of reminders, here's a quick tour of what is available. These lists are hardly meant to be complete or to fit everyone's individual preferences. But they are examples of pleasures within reach for most people – and unfortunate reminders that the sensory environment most of us take to be normal is in fact a source of sensory pain.

Pleasing Sights: The sea. The night sky. Green plants. Well-chosen furniture and wall colours, clothing, tableware. Warm indoor lighting.

Pleasing Sounds: Music of one's own choosing. Bird song. Waves.

Pleasing Scents: Flowers. Herbs and spices such as lavender, nutmeg, vanilla. The natural scent of certain healthy humans.

Pleasing Tastes: Meats, cheeses, fruits and vegetables. Wines and other fermented and distilled drinks. Bread. Teas, coffee and cacao.

Pleasing Touch: Silk, velvet, leather. The fur of animals. Smooth skin. Well-shaped tools and instruments.

Painful Sights: Slums and ghettos. Plastic toys. Institutional interiors, including hospital corridors, schools and transportation hubs.

Painful Sounds: Sirens, car horns, traffic. Other people's music. Dogs barking. Babies crying. Dripping water.

Painful Scents: Mould. Excrement. Most chemical
   perfumes and cleaning products. Rotting garbage.
Painful Tastes: Spoiled food. Artificial flavours. Overly
   sweet or salty food.
Painful Touch: Scratchy, sweaty, too-tight clothing. Poorly
   functioning utensils. Concrete flooring.

One way to upgrade your environment immediately at virtually
no cost is to remove every plastic bottle, tube or jar with a written label from your line of sight in your bathroom and kitchen.
The semantic clutter will disappear, along with many products
you don't currently use and probably never will.

Nevertheless, an apparent difficulty in trying to live an
Epicurean life is that sensory pleasures often come at a high
price. The best foodstuffs and perfumes, the most luxurious
textures and the most beautiful furnishings and surroundings
are rarer and considerably more expensive than fast food, cheap
scent, polyester clothing, life in a noisy urban environment and
activities carried on in public spaces built with no aesthetic
considerations in mind. Many people, even those in prosperous
democratic societies, do not have enough money to live lives
relatively free of persecution, anxiety and deprivation. They
cannot afford to buy flowers or visit the seashore, and their
sensory environments, by the above standards, are distinctly
unpleasant. For the Epicurean, both the identification of pleasure with expensive luxury and the painfulness of economic
deprivation raise concerns that philosophy must address.

The question for most of us where the care of the self is
concerned is not 'Can I get the absolute best for myself?' but
'Can I improve my sensory environment relative to the level it's
at now?' Although we have only imperfect control over the
sensory environment, and although painful stimuli abound in

our lives, we can usually do something more to avoid the painful ones and increase our exposure to sources of sensory pleasure.

Although it is a cliché to say that the best things in life are free, the conclusion that the most enjoyable things in life do not in principle require either sophisticated technologies or large outlays of cash has been echoed by psychologists investigating human happiness. Surveyed people reported as the most enjoyable activities of their day: intimate relations, socialising after work, relaxing, dinner, lunch and exercising. Commuting, work and childcare ranked low on the list of enjoyable activities – a point I'll return to later in connection with work and family life. While a remarkable array of desires for new objects and experiences can be stimulated in human beings, income and assets above a certain threshold have been found to have no bearing on subjective well-being, with the exception that people are sensitive to relative differences and are disposed to judge their own value to others by reference to what others have and how they are paid.

But most of us are at least mildly irrational in one way or another. Some who can't afford it splash out on purchases that do not really bring much pleasure. Others who have plenty of money behave as though they do not deserve to have beauty and comfort around them and scrimp, sacrificing quality in food and drink. They may feel subconsciously that sacrifices in these departments are redemptive, that they are showing, earning or recovering moral virtue by saving money in these areas. They are waiting to upgrade their living standards until the children move out ... until they get a boyfriend ... or until they win the lottery. Although deferring improvements and enjoyments may be prudent, often people could make beneficial changes now. They could afford it, or they could afford it if they reorganised their priorities in a reasonable way. But they accept a dreary environment and their own exertions as punishment for imaginary, unknown crimes of which they feel themselves to be guilty, or as preparing the way for a glorious future that will in fact never come if they don't take action.

Banish these superstitions, says the Epicurean. You don't deserve punishment, and you don't deserve to treat yourself either. It isn't a question of deserving at all.

As Epicureanism is a philosophy of, among other things, food, let's talk about food. Epicurus himself claimed to be satisfied with only a little bread, cheese, water and diluted wine, but such a diet cannot be recommended. It is monotonous and, in fact, unhealthy; I suspect it was supplemented with olives, grapes, figs, cabbages and other produce in season, though probably not with much meat or even fish, which Epicurus considered a luxury. The modern Western diet, by contrast, consists of easily chewable, year-round available, high-calorie substances, generally low in vitamins, trace elements, enzymes and beneficial bacteria and high in salt and sugar. Modern Americans consume an average of only thirty different foods, with 60 per cent of vegetable consumption going on potatoes, lettuce and tomato. Starches such as bread, rice and pasta figure heavily, and sweets and sweetened drinks may be eaten or drunk at every meal and in between meals.

The culturally mainstream diet is conducive to diabetes, tooth decay and cardiovascular disease. So why do people choose it? They are in a hurry, the food is cheap, familiar and filling, and its effects on health will not show up immediately. But they are harming themselves and likely creating pain and trouble for spouses and children, so the issue is one of both prudence and ethics. In keeping with the general tenor of Epicurus's recommendations, the Epicurean way of life today involves avoiding the mainstream diet and choosing, whenever possible, colourful food you prepare yourself from raw ingredients, avoiding canned, cured, bottled and prepared food and drinks, and not using more than a pound of salt and a pound or two of sugar in a year. There are many reasons to go to a restaurant rather than stay at home, but few restaurants can cook better than the average person who owns a cookbook and who has time, certainly not in a healthier and more economical fashion.

Going to restaurants can be pleasurable and occasionally memorable. They offer a tranquil or bustling ambience and interesting décor, the chance to try out new or favoured items on the menu, the opportunity to observe other members of the species in their often well-thought-out costumes, and to eavesdrop on their conversations, while being spared menu planning, shopping and washing up. Friendships ripen in restaurants. The Epicurean will respect both sets of values – nutrition and taste on the one hand, and entertainment and escape from routine on the other – and try to keep them in balance.

The reflective Epicurean will consider honestly what purchases have really brought pleasure and which ones were not worth the effort or the outlay. Think of the ones you don't regret: perhaps you really do love your yoghurt foot wash, or your new beige sofa, or your fancy chronometer. Think of the purchases you *do* regret: the exercise machine you never use, the designer sheets that now look just like ordinary sheets. Has your great big car brought you the happiness you hoped for? Did the wild party weekend at the resort leave you with fond memories of the wonderful time you had? Does your heart lift when you open your bureau drawer and see that glittery pair of socks? If so, it was money well spent. And take some time to reflect on whether housework and handyperson activities bring you joy or the reverse. While many people enjoy doing things around the house, there can be pleasure in *not* doing things. Perhaps you should pay for a housekeeper, or an ironing service, or have a professional paint the room instead of you.

Psychologists have discovered and commented on the 'hedonistic paradox', the 'hedonic treadmill' and the 'hedonic set point'. The paradox is that directly pursuing pleasure, especially by following a deadline-driven magazine writer's or sly advertiser's recommendations, is not the way to get pleasure. Pleasure arises as a by-product when we are engaged by what we are doing or experiencing, and people like to do and are engaged by different things.

Many people find playing a musical instrument highly pleasurable. Fresh flowers and green plants in a room bring pleasure to most people. But grimly signing up for the music lessons you detested as a child and resolutely setting out for the shops this morning to purchase plants and flowers in order to become happy later today probably will not work. Further, the person who directly pursues pleasure may get a temporary lift that quickly wears off, leaving him or her bored and depleted and seeking the next pleasure high. Set-point theory tells us that people's subjective happiness level is basically set for life and that the needle budges only temporarily in response to gratifying events, such as winning a prize or getting a raise, before falling back to wherever it was.

Has modern psychology proved that Epicureanism is a useless philosophy? By no means. Enormous numbers of people read advice columns, buy self-help books and visit mental-health practitioners because they are suffering or just not enjoying life. The hope is that knowledge and understanding can improve the situation. In some cases, the therapeutic method involves the minute examination of the sufferer's childhood, or the interpretation of their personal dreams, or the treatment of their fears by desensitisation using pictures or other media.

In other cases, however, the therapeutic method is essentially philosophical. From their own experience and from the accounts they have read about in casebooks and heard from their patients, authors and practitioners provide insight into how reality is structured, how the social world generally works and what usually happens when a person follows one policy rather than another. They teach the patient to reflect more consciously on patterns of choice and avoidance and, as Epicurus would advise, to show prudence in anticipating likely outcomes. Finally – while keeping a proper professional distance – they furnish a form of friendship, by giving the patient understanding and intimacy. Although this is not true friendship because it is not the reciprocal sharing of understanding and intimacy, and because it is paid for, it is ideally based on trust and sympathy.

So, although the discoveries of modern experimental psychology might seem to undermine hedonism as a philosophy for life, therapeutic practices in modern clinical psychology strongly support Epicurus's version of it. If set-point theory were the whole truth, therapy would be 100 per cent useless; no one could really be made happier and the entire profession ought to hang its head in shame at extracting money on an ongoing basis from vulnerable and incurable patients. Conversely, if therapy isn't 100 per cent useless when it comes to enabling people to live better lives, that is because it rests on sound methods, the most successful of which may actually be philosophical.

When not raising paradoxes and problems for hedonism, the research psychologists who work on this topic advise us to pursue pleasurable experiences rather than buying things. This is generally good advice, but isn't the purpose of any purchase to have a good experience with the thing? And isn't buying things intrinsically a pleasurable experience for everyone who doesn't hate shopping?

These points are well taken. But it helps to remember that buying a lipstick and glittery socks may be considerably more fun than possessing or even wearing the lipstick and the socks. Purchasing a prettily packaged, nice-smelling apricot and honey product can be more fun than actually covering your whole body with a sticky emulsion. If you want to spend money on these things, keep it in mind that the enjoyment you derive may be limited to the moment of purchase.

Like any position, hedonism – the doctrine that pleasure is the only good and pain the only evil – can be pushed to absurd and untenable extremes never intended by the Epicureans, past or present. Imagine, for example, that a new drug is invented that, for pennies a day, and within easy reach of all, can keep those who take it in a dawn-till-dusk state of bliss, yet able to perform the most repetitive and degrading work in objectively hideous conditions, among rats, fleas and cockroaches. Already there are drugs taken by soldiers on combat missions that enable them to kill in a state of gleeful excitement without painful scruples. Would you consider yourself to have a pleasant life if you were in the first situation? If not, it is clear that by pleasure we need not understand a subjective feeling of bliss bearing no intrinsic relation to the surrounding circumstances. Nor can the Epicurean, for reasons to be explored in the next chapter, regard the existence of drugs that facilitate cheerful killing without conscience – unlike drugs that can relieve one's own acute or incurably chronic physical pain – as a boon to humanity. The ups and downs of addiction, according to the testimony of addicts and those who live close to them, do not contribute to a pleasant life either.

DON'T SUFFER IN SILENCE!

As well as giving you permission to upgrade, prudently, Epicureanism encourages you to deal with your pains, avoiding martyrdom. We are often told that we should ignore petty annoyances. The Epicurean takes the opposite view. That hangnail is bothering you? Go snip it off right now. The hall light is burned out? Get the stepladder. You have too many keys and can't tell which is which? Colour code them. Your children say hurtful things to you? Ask them to stop.

The worst conditions to be in are those of searing or stabbing pains, high fever, aching limbs, nausea, a throbbing tooth, deafening noises, gnawing hunger. On the psychological side, the worst conditions are hopelessness, terror, jealousy and gnawing anxiety. Some conditions of life are just unpleasurable, though not as terrible as the extremes of physical and mental pain just mentioned: these include being stressed, bored, tired and chilly. These states of body and mind can spoil one's life, or at least the present moment, and prevent one enjoying the good things that are available.

When your shoes pinch, it is hard to enjoy the architecture you travelled all those miles to see. Above all, resist superstition and the temptation to turn pain into moral virtue. A long tradition, not only of Western philosophy but of many other philosophies and religions, teaches that suffering is good and earns one compensation in the future or rewards in another life. People were urged for centuries to endure their hardships and injustices and assured that all would turn out well for them in the end. And at times we are too tired, too distracted or just too lazy to make things better. Doubtless you have pinching shoes, a jacket that makes you look frumpy, a bedspread in a colour you don't like. Why do you still wear or use these things? Is it because these shoes are beautiful and you think you look wonderful in them? Because the jacket is at least warm and the bedspread has sentimental value? No: it is probably because you paid good money for them and are punishing yourself for a bad choice by putting up with them. This is called getting full use out of them, or until I find something better.

For the Epicurean, this attitude leads to a painful and expensive life.

Get rid of them. Cut your losses. If you can do without, so much the better. If not, the time to find something better is now. You have learned something about choice and avoidance, and will hesitate in the future before wasting money on anything that does not both delight you now and show excellent prospects for delighting you in the future. To be sure, very promising items can turn out to be mistakes, but it is rare that something you thought was wonderful, not just OK, when you first bought it turns out to be a major disappointment later.

Avoiding pain is more important for overall satisfaction with life than pursuing pleasure, and there are many unnecessary sources of trouble and vexation in our lives. Cars and pets are good examples. Some people need to own a car, but for others it's just a convention to have one, and those who have disburdened themselves of a car are no longer bothered by having to negotiate to buy them, or by maintaining, repairing, inspecting, licensing, refuelling and reselling them. Interaction with pets can bring a lot of pleasure. The devotion people show to their dogs and cats is sufficient proof of this, but if you don't feel you have enough time in the day and you have pets or are thinking you should get a pet, think hard about the time, effort and expense of pet ownership.

Going to the doctor, and taking family members and pets to the doctor, is always time consuming and often expensive. A poster advertising a walk-in clinic in America, where any visit to a doctor involves paperwork and usually money, asks, 'Why wait 48 hours to see a doctor for a 24-hour virus?' As they used to tell us in maths class, all the information you need to solve the problem is contained in the question. Doctors themselves will tell you that there is no point in going to the doctor unless you have developed a new and alarming symptom or have been unable for days to carry out necessary or enjoyable activities. You can check your rashes on the Internet; some are dangerous, most are not. Most things are better in the morning.

The advice to wait it out does not apply to unusual symptoms you have not experienced before, or to severe or chronic pain, an important topic that I will discuss in Chapter 8 (pages 123–145). Our longer lives condemn us to worn-out joints and crumbling bones. If you have severe or chronic pain, *do* go to the doctor, and do insist that it be diagnosed and treated. Women in particular often have difficulty in getting their symptoms acknowledged and investigated.

The world of work offers fewer opportunities for choice and avoidance, but there is usually something you can do. If you are an Epicurean manager, you can help in small and perhaps even large ways to make the time spent at work more pleasant and less stressful. The manager in my last job ensured that there was a large bowl of fruit next to the coffee machine in the staff room. Walking into the room and seeing oranges, apples, bananas and plums was pleasurable. The manager in my current job has assured us that the sky will not fall if employees don't email on the weekends or after 5:30 p.m. The business of the department will get done regardless. Meetings are no longer scheduled at the end of the day but in the afternoon, so that people can get home to their children and cook dinner.

If your job brings you little satisfaction, think it over. How much money do you really need? Shorter work hours have been repeatedly shown to reduce stress and to result in a more equal and satisfying division of household tasks. They also leave more time for socialising, volunteer work and political action.

As noted earlier, there can be suffering for a good cause. Mary pays the bills and John cleans the refrigerator. It is tiresome but prevents future unpleasantness. Sam could quickly relieve his minor headache by taking a powerful opiate he buys on the street, but he doesn't want to get involved with dealers. Triumphing over adversity can bring pleasure that outweighs the pain of adversity. But banging your head against a wall or a ball, or anything else, for any reason, is imprudent, regardless of the pleasant sensation you get when you stop. It is really hard on your material brain, which you need for thinking, feeling and experiencing.

But life is complicated. While it is easy to send those shoes to the charity shop, and not impossible to press for or initiate changes at work, other people cause many degrees and varieties of pain that are confusing and sometimes immobilising.

Most letters to advice columns take the following form: 'I am really bothered by how my girlfriend/husband/boss is treating me. This is causing me a lot of agony. Should I say something, or should I end it/leave him/quit? Should I just keep my mouth shut and grin and bear it? I like/love my girlfriend/husband/job, and I am hoping things will improve.'

This formula – the dilemma formula – appears over and over. The answers given by the expert will be versions of 'Obviously you should ...' or else 'No one can make this decision for you.' Usually, it is the latter, and the letter writer may well feel disappointed. The whole point of writing to the newspaper was to get clear, objective direction that ensures against regret down the road. But the fact is, we cannot ensure against regret.

Students of sociology, following Albert Hirschman, are aware that there are three possible responses to the dilemmas posed by deteriorating relationships, including those indicated by the letter writers: exit, voice and loyalty. The disgruntled or suffering party can leave, sacrificing what benefits there are in the relationship, but avoiding a confrontation; they can protest against their mistreatment vigorously and explicitly enough to be noticed; or they can put up with the situation because there are really no better alternatives out there.

The Epicurean cannot tell you, any more than the average newspaper columnist can, exactly what to do to get out of a painful situation, just as he can't tell you exactly how to get more pleasure into your life. But he encourages you to do something: to make a graceful and quiet exit, to summon up the courage for a confrontation that may or may not turn out the way you want it to, or to make a deliberate decision that the situation just has to be endured.

Regardless of the trouble other people can cause for us, Epicurus believed close human relationships to be the greatest source of pleasure in life. 'Of the things which wisdom provides for the blessedness of one's whole life, by far the greatest is the possession of friendship.' Friendship offers opportunities for shared attention, a distinctive aspect of human behaviour that other animals display only fleetingly, and for the full use of our powers of humour, aesthetic appreciation and speculation. Young children point out objects of interest to others even before they can speak. As teenagers, both boys and girls develop a powerful capacity for emotional intimacy and dependency extending outside the family. As adults, friends see films together, lend one another books, travel or take walks together, speculate about world events and gossip about their common acquaintances. They help with projects requiring more than one pair of hands, and even if they are rarely or never needed in a medical or financial emergency, there is security, Epicurus comments, in knowing that they would help.

Unlike Aristotle, Epicurus did not moralise about the criteria to be employed in picking friends. Indeed, reflective choice does not usually enter into forming a friendship; people find the conversation and companionship of certain people rewarding, others not so much, and fall into association with them without feeling the need to tick boxes. But choice and avoidance do have a role to play, insofar as cultivating a friendship takes thought and planning. Someone has to initiate, Epicurus noted, and not everyone who bids for a particular friendship is successful.

The loss of a friend to death or relocation, or as the result of a quarrel, is painful in a way that the gradual attrition of a friendship is not. Although impermanence is a feature of all complex objects and relations for the Epicurean, we have a sense of how long particular things ought to last, as I will explain in Chapter 8 (pages 125–45). When they give out prematurely, grief is the appropriate emotion to experience. Prudence does not, however, urge us to forego friendship on the grounds that we may someday be subject to a loss. We live among many fragile and semi-fragile things, and friendship is only one of them.

The Pleasure Merchants

The Epicurean believes that we naturally avoid and seek to remedy mental and physical pain and welcome pleasure in a prudential fashion. We should do so without feeling either guilty or deserving. Too much prudence, however, is as inadvisable as too little. Whenever they are offered by profit-making organisations, both insurance taken out to cover material goods and investigative medical procedures are frequently oversold. Impulsive actions – eloping with your lover, making an immediate offer on your dream house, quitting your job and contacting a head-hunter – can bring enormous satisfaction.

At the same time, it is important to remember that, unlike the ancients, we live in a commercially and psychologically sophisticated society. Although for the Epicurean first-person experience is the touchstone of truth, first impressions are not always reliable. The people selling us things, from lipsticks and cars to detergents and appliance insurance, know how to appeal to our senses as well as our hopes, fears and anxieties. All advertisements play on these sensory and emotional keyboards. For self-defence, it is helpful to ask of each tempting advertisement or offer you see what hope or fear or anxiety (and all hope is a kind of fear) it is arousing. The pleasure merchants have done extensive research, and they know from their sales figures what kind of appeal will move products off the shelves. But they have only a pretend interest in our happiness. The up-for-it model does not come with the car, and the car will not help you to get her. The woman on the box did not use the hair dye in the box and you will not look anything like that when you are done.

Philosophers are no different, you might be thinking. They, too, are selling something by tapping into our desires and vulnerabilities. For why should the enlightenment and well-being of people they have never met matter in the least to them?

It would be difficult to exonerate philosophers entirely from this charge, so approach philosophy with caution. An important difference, however, between philosophical ideas and arguments and other products on offer is that philosophy, like other forms of teaching and healing, is a vocation. The physician, the mathematics or history lecturer, the baseball coach and the philosopher are earning a living by imparting what they hope is useful knowledge and by employing skilled technologies, material and psychological. With some conspicuous exceptions, they do so with little hope or intention of amassing fame or fortune. Do not underestimate the extent of genuine altruism and commitment in the world. Further, the philosopher rarely tells you just what you want to hear, and even more rarely affirms all your desires as deserving gratification.

6

MORALITY AND OTHER PEOPLE

*The justice of nature is a pledge of reciprocal usefulness ...
neither to harm one another nor to be harmed ... Justice was
not a thing in its own right, but [exists] in mutual dealings in
whatever places there [is] a pact about neither harming one
another nor being harmed.*

Epicurus

*It is impossible to live pleasantly without living prudently,
honourably and justly, and impossible to live prudently,
honourably and justly without living pleasantly.*

Epicurus

Philosophical ethics has a good deal to say about the difference between real needs and desires on the one hand, and desires induced by manipulation on the other. It urges us to discriminate between fleeting pleasures and more durable pleasures, and to think hard and courageously about the management of personal risk. But philosophical ethics has another important goal: to explore the question of how to treat other people and why we ought to treat them that way; how it is right or just or fair to treat them.

Epicureanism is not a philosophy of pure selfishness. The teaching that pleasure is the only real good and pain the only real evil goes for everyone, not just for me. And it is obvious that *my* enjoyment of *my* pleasures can have adverse effects on *you* or on others, causing you or them pain, or depriving you or them of pleasures.

MORALITY VS PRUDENCE

Prudence puts limits on my enjoyments and forces a certain amount of pain on me now, in the expectation that the overall sum of pain and pleasure will work out favourably for the pleasure side over the interval under consideration. Prudence is accordingly central to the part of ethics dealing with the care of the self.

Let's now get realistic. Isn't it often prudent to be immoral? One way for me to prevent or lessen painful experiences and to increase my own pleasure is to impose burdens on you or to deprive you of pleasures you would otherwise have. Lying – for example, denying that I reported scurrilous gossip about you or broke the TV antenna or let the cat out – can preserve me from unpleasant accusations, reproaches and retaliation. Saying I have a prior engagement when I don't can enable me to avoid a disagreeable encounter. Stealing from the grocery store can assuage my gnawing hunger. Supporting industries that are cruel to workers or that hurt animals can provide me with nice or warm clothes. Stealing from the jewellery counter can add to my cache of pretty objects. Acting on lusts forbidden by laws or codes can bring sexual gratification. Getting a rival skier assassinated could boost my chances at winning the Olympic Gold Medal, which might make me very happy, at least for a while.

No matter how much moral theorists try to persuade us that the delights of virtuous behaviour outweigh all possible gratifications from the common vices of dishonesty, theft and general irresponsibility, we have reason to be sceptical. If there are good reasons not to lie, steal, act on illegal or inappropriate desires, cooperate with exploiters or kill people for advancement, this can't be because there is no satisfaction or reduction of pain to be gained for me by acting in this way.

If there is no God to punish me for cruelty and deception or to reward me for good behaviour, why shouldn't I do whatever seems most advantageous for me at the moment, provided I can get away with it? Who or what is to tell me what I ought to do, or may do, or shouldn't do? To put it simply, prudence or self-interest can clash directly with what we usually think of as moral norms. If life is strictly finite, if we are here by chance, if life has no cosmic meaning or purpose, only the meanings and purposes we create, how can any behaviour be forbidden or permitted or required of me? The Epicureans were well aware of this problem and approached it as follows.

Morality, for Epicurus, is a set of harm-reducing conventions. Remembering the nature–convention distinction, we could say that the pursuit of pleasure and avoidance of pain, the care of the self, is natural. What I ought to choose and avoid, where purely self-regarding actions are concerned, depends on my tastes and preferences, and only requires correction through prudence – moderate attention to the longer-term consequences for me. Morality, which Epicurus refers to as 'justice', is similar in some ways but different in others. Both prudence and morality put some limits on my immediate enjoyment and force a certain amount of pain or deprivation on the 'me' of right now. As the beneficiary of prudence is not my present self but a future self, the beneficiary of my moral action is not myself at all but another person or another set of people entirely. Its corrective purpose is to ensure that what *I* gain by my choices and avoidances does not impose an unacceptable amount of pain on *you*, or deprive you in an unacceptable way of pleasures you would otherwise enjoy.

The Marquis de Sade notoriously defended everything he proposed to do to his victims on the grounds that he was following nature and that pleasure was the supreme good. This was an obvious misappropriation of Epicurean philosophy. The Marquis's imaginary victims, though they were subjected to a large dose of libertine pseudo-Epicurean theory in the novels he composed in prison, were treated neither as friends, nor as strangers entitled to justice. His actual victims probably escaped the philosophy lectures, but they suffered abuses no actual follower of Epicurus could have sanctioned.

All human societies – the selfishness and sadism of the Ik, an African tribe wholly demoralised by a two-year famine, notwithstanding – have rules governing the allocation of pain and pleasure, and there is considerable overlap. Most moral codes in some way restrain aggression, deception and fraud, insults and damage to reputation, and sexual behaviour. They are conventional insofar as they are based on *estimates* of permissible and impermissible harms. The codes evolve as estimates of who is harmed and by how much change in response to new information and to the adoption of different perspectives.

This might seem an anaemic and at the same time rather grim way of looking at morality. Isn't morality about generosity, kindness, honesty and goodwill? Isn't morality about our real obligations to others, and so about more than a set of conventions? A long tradition of moral philosophy insists that 'rights', 'duties' and 'obligations' belong to the very fabric of the universe. Many philosophers today believe that moral facts about how to treat other humans and animals are like mathematical truths, that they can be discovered by reason and analytical thinking. But why should I care about any of this if the immediate beneficiary is not me? Prudence is in my self-interest if I look far enough ahead, but is morality also in my self-interest?

The Epicurean position is that kindness and generosity to friends flows naturally from your affection for them and does not need to be instilled by convention. You pick your friend up from the airport; he helps you put your bookcases together; you may bring one another presents for the pleasure of picking them out and offering them. But your spontaneous helpfulness and goodwill towards your friends, the Epicurean maintains, has nothing to do with morality. By contrast, avoiding and preventing harm, especially to strangers, does not flow from warm and friendly feelings towards them. And there are massive benefits to be gained from deceiving people, using their labour, restricting their freedoms and taking their possessions, provided that they don't realise what is happening or are powerless to resist. This can and does occur even between friends.

Because the Epicurean believes that all sentient animals do naturally seek pleasure and avoid pain, and because humans are notably clever and conniving, he is realistic about the need for moral conventions to curb and correct what comes naturally. Without explicit moral teaching about how not to treat other people, without the development of the learner's conscience, people would behave more opportunistically and harmfully than they do. And because retaliation against those who have harmed us is also natural, but leads to never-ending and sometimes bloody feuds, we need institutions that administer punishment fairly and evenly, after taking into consideration the circumstances and effects of the offence and the response to it.

MORAL TRUTH AND MORAL PROGRESS

The Epicurean regards 'moral duties', 'moral obligations', 'moral prohibitions' and 'moral laws' as existing at the opposite end of the reality scale from atoms and void. They depend on human needs and interests, and they change and evolve for two important reasons.

One reason is that societies evolve new forms of organisation and new technologies. Morality has to play catch-up as clever humans discover new ways to deceive, use, coerce and rob one other that were not previously available. As Lucretius observed, the invention of metal introduced new forms of warfare and new forms of labour. Most inventions in our history have been used both to help and to harm. The invention of print permitted mass education, but also propaganda, misinformation and manipulation. The Industrial Revolution cheapened many goods but condemned many people to monotonous, gruelling labour for barely enough money to keep them alive and on the job.

These examples can be multiplied at length. Most recently, the Internet, robotics and reproductive technologies have raised moral problems because of the potential for one person to harm another by using them. Social media brings people into warm and useful contact and also enables them to heap verbal abuse on one another, to make upsetting threats, and to shame and blackmail them. New moral norms have to be worked out through discussion and debate by the public, including philosophers and journalists, and new forms of conscience instilled by educators. These norms, too, are subject to revision in the light of changing circumstances.

When we declare that some moral norm or other is absolute – for example, the prohibition on killing people for financial gain – we express the conviction that no change in our circumstances could ever result in a change to this norm as a result of informed debate. It can feel satisfying to express such general commitments, but it is important to consider whether we respect the commitment in our actions. Out of ignorance or hypocrisy we may well contribute to or vote for legislators who support policies of, for example, environmental deregulation, that result in people being killed for financial gain. Our ancestors saw no problem with attacking foreign nations for their economic resources, and some of the harder heads in the so-called defence industry seem to have no problem with this either, even if they would profess horror at the idea of killing the next-door neighbours for financial gain.

The second reason morality changes and evolves beside technological innovation is that we learn more about the world. Superstition is eradicated by active investigation and the discovery of real (and the elimination of imaginary) causal mechanisms. The fear, repulsion and anxiety surrounding menstruation and homosexuality have diminished as we have acquired a more scientific understanding of their biological significance. People's eyes are opened, thanks to the analysis of economists and sociologists, enabling us to see how organisational decisions are made, and who extracts a benefit from taking advantage of the weakness or ignorance of others.

The Epicurean of today has respect for morality, even while he regards it as needing adjustment to current circumstances and as revisable in the light of experience. And just as the sacrifices of prudence when it comes to long-term planning are not always warranted because they interfere too much with my present enjoyment, a society may decide to allow some harms to some people because the benefits to others are greater. Permitting automobiles on the road harms those people who lose their lives or get maimed in crashes, but we judge the helps to the majority to outweigh the harms to this unfortunate minority. Taxing the wealthy at a higher rate, although it does not deprive them either of necessities or of the means of satisfying most of their desires, can annoy or anger them because losing something one had is experienced as harmful. But these pains experienced by the wealthy are morally acceptable because of the much greater helps to the poor that their funds can provide. Because

Epicureans put no stock in the notion of individual desert, they are unmoved by arguments that the wealthy deserve their wealth and the poor do not deserve to partake of it.

WHY BE MORAL?

To the question, 'Why should I be moral?' the Epicureans gave the following answers: first, because you understand why, in light of human nature and the multitude of possibilities life offers for harming others, morality is a necessary human invention. Second, because if you believe current moral norms are outdated and based on wrong information, you can work to change them. Third, because you live in a society that cares about morality, you will be punished if you act immorally and are discovered. The last reason, which makes moral conformity prudent, needs some discussion.

Offences ranging from rudeness and uncooperativeness to cheating, fraud, larceny, physical assault and murder are punished in one or both of two ways: informally, by social disapproval, verbal criticism and the withdrawal of friendship; formally, by inflicting pain and inconvenience on the offender, typically through fines or imprisonment, sometimes by forfeit of life. The knowledge that the mechanisms of punishment exist helps to keep us in line, insofar as we are averse to pain. These considerations, the Epicureans thought, should be enough for anyone with a modicum of basic good heartedness and rationality. And a person who is not persuaded will nevertheless be subjected to the institutions of a morally concerned society for the detection and punishment of moral wrongs.

The eventual discovery of your crimes is all but inevitable, Epicurus maintained. Even if your offences are not immediately brought to light, your conscience will gnaw at you and you will live in the painful fear that they will be. The terrors of Hell, Lucretius maintains, 'do not exist and cannot exist anywhere at all. But in life people are tortured by a fear of punishment as cruel as their crimes.' He goes on to recite a list of Roman criminal punishments, including being thrown into a dungeon, tossed over a precipice and burned with hot pitch or torches.

How effective such procedures actually were in deterring crime is an empirical question, and how far it is permissible to go to deter crime is a moral question. Our modern prisons are ghastly places, rife with sadism and abuse, that are neither effective nor morally justifiable. We need not endorse the particular forms punishment takes in the modern world to see the necessity of pursuing responses to criminality that make its occurrence less likely.

WHAT'S DIFFERENT ABOUT EPICUREAN MORALITY?

The Epicurean conception of morality can be contrasted with theological ethics, with moral realism and with Stoicism.

Theological ethics is 'top down'. It posits a divine legislator who has wisely established permanent rules for human behaviour, such as those stated in various books of the Jewish-Christian Old Testament and the Islamic Koran, and who enforces them with punishments and rewards in this world and/ or the next. In this view, moral rules are learned from sacred texts and from the interpretations of these writings by a priestly elite. Although the rules, since they were first enunciated in the nomadic pastoral societies of the second millennium BCE, sometimes require interpretation in the light of new circumstances and knowledge, they are basically fixed for all time. For the Epicurean, this account is incompatible with her view of what actually exists, her view of how human history has developed and with her epistemology, which does not recognise a special category of sacred text.

Moral realism posits moral facts or moral truths, some of which, like some mathematical truths, have already been discovered, while others await our discovery. For example, it is sometimes said that it was always true that 'slavery is wrong', just as it was always true that $2 + 2 = 4$, even at the time of the Big Bang, though it took many millennia to discover this (and one would certainly not learn the truth about slavery from the Old Testament). And it might be thought that we will one day discover whether it is obligatory to be a vegetarian and whether torture is morally permissible – the obligation and the permission either exist now or they don't.

For the Epicurean, our future experience and reflection on experience should and will determine our decisions and direct our practices. But our practices will change, not because we have discovered a pre-existing but previously unknown fact or proved a moral theorem by analysis, but because we have had to change our estimates of who is harmed or helped and by how much, and our views about whose harms and helps matter.

Finally, Epicurean morality can be compared with the influential Stoic theory of virtue. The four Stoic virtues were wisdom, temperance, courage and justice. For the Stoic, morality not only requires the sacrifice of self-interest, it can also require the infliction of pain and even death for the sake of principle alone. Justice might demand the execution of one's own son, as courage might demand a willingness to die in battle for one's country. Neither compassion nor benevolence to others belong to the Stoic virtues.

The Epicurean agrees that wise, courageous and just actions may be those we ought to perform and that temperance is better than dissolution. But she sees wisdom as pleasant and useful rather than moral. The pursuit of knowledge and the adoption of temperate habits are in the interests of the individual as sources of long-term pleasure. Where courage and justice, the other-regarding virtues, are concerned, she has some further doubts. Stoicism was and is still especially prized in military contexts. And when courage involves inflicting fear, pain and death on other human beings, and putting oneself in the way of pain, fear and death, it is not a quality the Epicurean can admire. He can see no moral goodness in my sacrificing my own security and possibly my own health and life for the economic or geopolitical interests of others. Patriotism is not to be found in nature, and blind allegiance to a particular country needs to be questioned even when it swells the heart and brings joy. Is my country really so admirable in all respects, and are all its policies deserving of unconditional support? Individual and collective courage in politics is entirely different from individual and collective courage in battle.

Must the Epicurean be a pacifist for the sake of morality? Lucretius was clear that causes of war are greed and ambition. But the Epicurean can be anti-war without being a pacifist. Epicurus recognised that policing is necessary and may require the use of force, even lethal force. International agreements, in an Epicurean conception, are needed to legitimate the use of force abroad, which can only be directed, like policing, to crime prevention, and not to advancing the national interest. When innocent people, including bystanders, are harmed or killed in police actions, the police are called to account, and the same ought to be true whenever civilians are attacked in the name of international peacekeeping.

The Epicurean believes that laws that are accepted as just in a particular society condemn some of its citizens to misery in the form of hunger, disease, squalor and abuse. These include import restrictions and laws governing corporate behaviour; for example, those allowing corporations to set drug prices as they wish. The so-called criminal justice system condemns more than two million Americans, about a third of them young and black, to a horrific prison experience that has rarely set anyone on a better path. We should not make idols of the Stoic virtues or of the concept of justice without reflecting on whether particular acts of so-called justice are conducive to human welfare or not.

7

BEWARE OF LOVE!

*[S]o in love, lovers are deluded by Venus with images: no
matter how intently they gaze at the beloved body, they
cannot sate their eyes; nor can they remove anything from the
velvety limbs that they explore with roving, uncertain hands.*

Lucretius

*Perhaps his mistress has thrown out an ambiguous word and
left it embedded in his passionate heart, where it burns like
living fire; or perhaps he fancies that her eyes are wandering
too freely, or that she is ogling some other man, while he
detects in her face the trace of a smile.*

Lucretius

So far, I've explained how the Epicurean thinks about relationships with one's present self, one's future self and with the friends and strangers to whom we give moral consideration. But what about romantic and sexual relationships, inside and outside marriage?

On the basis of the writings we know about, Epicurus maintained a level-headed attitude towards such relationships throughout his entire life. Lucretius's treatment of romantic passion, which I will get to shortly, is by contrast impressively thorough. As he was well aware, romantic infatuation, when all is going well, is undoubtedly the happiest state a human being can enjoy, more pleasurable than the enjoyment of wealth or fame, or even the relief and joy one feels on recovering from a serious illness. Correspondingly, the loss or alienation, even the fear of the loss or alienation, of an adored partner brings psychological anguish inferior only to that of the loss of a child to death. Despair at not getting the one you wanted, 'lying in bonds of love, torn by winged creatures', as Lucretius describes it, can shatter us, or lead to murder and suicide. His suicide in his mid-forties seems to have been in some way romantically motivated, a most unusual fate for a philosopher, and one that also aroused much scornful commentary on the failures of Epicurean philosophy.

Please do not follow his example in this regard – I will give you reasons why not to kill yourself for love in the next chapter. But it is clear that if the gods had designed the world with human tranquillity in mind, they would not have outfitted us with the emotions and temperaments we actually possess. Like drug addiction, with which infatuation has a lot in common from a biochemical perspective, romantic love raises important questions of prudence and morality, insofar as it both affects our long-term interests and has effects on other people.

The Epicurean looks at the world realistically, though not cynically. She is, as always, attentive to the balance of pain and pleasure in intimate relations, to the distinction between the natural and the conventional, and to the role of imagination. If we can understand why intimate relations can be so troubled, as well as why they are so gratifying, we can perhaps escape some of the miseries to which we are otherwise prone. Remembering that new knowledge and new technologies are the basis of moral change, we can ask what is different today that makes certain old attitudes obsolete.

THE EPICUREAN EXCEPTION

The Epicurean school was the only ancient Greek or Roman philosophical school that allowed women to join, promoted friendship between men and women, and allowed women sexual freedom comparable to that of men. This was considered scandalous by Epicurus's philosophical opponents. He seems to have been constantly writing to women in affectionate terms, sending them books and inviting them to come and see him. Such behaviour is compatible with the kind of exploitation that frequently occurs in cults headed by a charismatic central figure, and we cannot be sure that these relationships were not based on more – and less – than mutual attraction and interest. But it is useful to remember that any quid pro quo must have been minimal: Epicurus could not have been offering great wealth, or film roles, or letters of recommendation, or career-furthering introductions.

Ancient Greek society, from which the Epicureans distanced themselves, restricted respectable married women – the wives of the people to whom most philosophy was addressed – to the home. They recognised three other classes of women: slaves, prostitutes and *hetairai*, a word usually translated as 'courtesans'. Women were conceptualised in terms of their functions for men. Wives were for forming family alliances and gestating male heirs and marriageable daughters; slaves were for manual work; prostitutes were for quick and cheap relief from tension; and courtesans were for intelligent conversation and emotionally intense relationships. Courtesans were often educated, literate and foreign. But they depended on men for subsistence or wealth acquisition, so were in effect long- or short-term 'mistresses'.

The Epicureans departed from the mainstream insofar as, at least in the writings available to us, they did not theorise about women as the possessions of men to be used for sex and domestic work. Unlike Plato in the *Republic*, they did not lay down schemes for the proper management of women for childbearing purposes. The most pleasing relationship a man could enter into was, in their view, a non-binding one with a woman whose education was comparable to his own, who was interested in the same ideas that he was and at leisure to discuss them, and who was not concerned with the supposed virtue of chastity. Neither wives nor prostitutes could fill this role; only the *hetairai*. Epicurean women, we might suppose, valued the attention paid by their male friends to their minds, their freedom from domestic servitude and the burden of having to uphold a reputation as chaste.

THE PAINS AND PLEASURES OF LOVE

Epicurus himself was not inclined to marry, though he left the choice open to his followers. Marriage, he believed, brought many cares and vexations with it, and children could be a nuisance. Lucretius, by contrast, took a more favourable perspective towards family life and children. He remarks that 'habit generates love' and that even a woman who is no great beauty 'easily accustoms a man to spend his life with her' if she is neat and obliging. He describes charmingly the affection of animal mothers for their offspring; and he sympathises with men who fear that the gods 'have prevented [them] from ever being called father by sweet children ... condemned to live a life cursed with sterility'. Their problem, he says, is physiological, not the effect of a curse, and it might be solved by a change in diet or by finding 'a partner of compatible make-up'. The same goes for women who are trying unsuccessfully to have children.

Nevertheless, Lucretius does put plain but pleasant wives and mothers who are loved for their familiarity into a different category from the women a man goes crazy over and from the women who go crazy over a man. For one thing, he states that wives should not move around too much when having sex, as this interferes with conception. The other kind of woman does appear to move around a lot. He notes that although a woman may sometimes feign pleasure in sex, 'often she is sincere' and ready to 'run the race of love to the goal'; other female animals obviously experience 'mutual delights'. Where sexual passion is concerned, he mixes satire with a form of awe. Passion is not a disease of the mind, as it is for the Stoics. It is nature's way of renewing life; if animals, including human beings, did not have powerful drives and attachments, their species would have died out. But the human lovers' fixation on one another leads to all sorts of problems, and they appear to the level-headed observer to be deranged. They are blind to one another's faults and deaf to the advice of others. Money is no object; they are reckless. They desperately try to merge their bodies into one, as impossible as this is.

The prudent person must recognise that love can be painful. One natural source of suffering is that human relations, when they are not being stage-managed by third parties, involve personal appraisals of potential partners, followed by choice or avoidance. Another person's looks, manners, conversation, scent or health status may trigger feelings of attraction, repulsion or indifference, and if attraction is one-sided it will be painful. For the Epicurean, this is a misfortune that has to be endured. Love is more often unrequited, or felt more strongly on one side than the other, than not. How can you relieve the pain of jealousy and uncertainty? When fixated on a person who does not care for you, Lucretius says, rather wisely, remind yourself that 'there are others like her; we have lived without her until now'. (This works for 'him', too.) Seek distractions by engaging in casual affairs while you get over the one who rejected you, and remind yourself of the least pleasing bodily functions of the one you obsess about. Epicurus was perhaps the first to discover the effectiveness of 'no contact'. 'If you take away the chance to see and talk and spend time with [the beloved],' he observes, 'then the passion of sexual love is dissolved.'

Even when based on mutual appreciation, passionate affairs rouse anxiety. Does the beloved want a future with me? Does the beloved want more from me than I can or am prepared to give them? Jealousy – if not about other competitors for the beloved's affections in the present, then about the beloved's past and whom and how many they were with – often becomes an issue in all relationships that are formed in adulthood. Some societies try to forestall these problems by marrying young, inexperienced persons to persons chosen by their parents and by imposing huge obstacles to divorce. These systems have their own disadvantages. They do not prevent both men and women from developing passionate attractions to others. The result is a double standard in which infidelities occur, but only women are punished for them.

Natural attraction, and even mutual attraction, may coexist with the appreciation that the other person is unavailable because they are married, or impoverished, or too old or too young, or they come from the wrong kind of family, or belong to the wrong religion. In a fully Epicurean society, no one is eligible or ineligible for such conventional reasons. Men's wealth and status does not make them especially attractive to women, and religion plays no role whatsoever, though a shared philosophy of life does. Obstructions and negative social judgements do not arise from supposed misalliances. But suppose I am an Epicurean in a non-Epicurean society, in which relationships are judged according to conventional standards. In that case, I must simply act prudently. Will the pleasure of requited love outweigh the pain caused by disapproval of the community? Can community opinion be changed without too much pain?

These questions became acute in the previous century for homosexuals who experienced mutual attraction, but whose desires were deemed unnatural and immoral when they were only unconventional and no more intrinsically harmful to anyone than heterosexual equivalents. From the empirical perspective, homosexual relationships, common in other animals, including insects, have been no obstacle to the survival of the various species, and even if male homosexuality has no 'Darwinian' benefit for the individual, by increasing the number of his descendants, it has been observed that it may have one for his female relatives.

Enormous suffering was caused by the superstition that homosexuality is an illness or else a wicked and criminal choice. Some pairs defied convention, keeping a low profile or joining together in subcultures that accepted other conventions, often being forced thereby to separate themselves from their families and unable to found families of their own. Others judged that defying the surrounding society would be too difficult and sacrificed their passions. In recent years, the conventions have changed. This occurred not only because scientific enquiry revealed homosexual love and desire to be natural in the animal kingdom as well as in the human world, but also because first-person testimony revealed that the joys and sorrows of requited and unrequited love were no different for homosexual than for heterosexual pairs.

SEXUAL MORALITY: MINIMISING HARM TO OTHERS

While it is common in our culture to think in terms of 'sexual morality', this was not a familiar concept for ancient philosophers outside the Judaeo-Christian-Islamic tradition. Unlike Jehovah, God and Allah, who were seen as having a detailed interest in people's intimate lives and as being in a position to lay down the law, Zeus or Jove had no authority in this regard. The Greek gods were more capricious and libertine than the mortals and did not propose to govern them by means of regulations, as opposed to occasional interventions. Although they observed rules and regulations governing incest and were disparaging of those who let themselves be used in a sexual manner, the ancients – including the Epicureans – generally thought of intimate relationships in terms of prudence and seemliness, rather than morality; that is, the potential for harm. Theirs is a useful perspective, even if we have since discovered that such relationships raise genuine moral issues, as well as issues of prudence.

In the case of natural attraction going beyond the boundaries of marriage, such issues inevitably arise. Loving attachments lasting months or years are natural for human beings; marriage, by contrast, is a nearly universal convention that is instituted and supported or coerced somewhat differently in every society, including hunter-gatherer cultures. Perfect lifelong sexual fidelity within the convention of marriage, on the part of both men and women, is at the same time the exception rather than the rule. Secrecy and hypocrisy, and the repression and slander of women in their division into madonnas and sluts implied in the double standard, arise from the conflict between nature and convention. If human beings were naturally monogamous, like swans, these troubles would not exist.

Epicurus's solution was to dispense with marriage and children and to carry on affairs with the women he liked. Lucretius's solution appears to have been a version of the applied double standard: courtesans were for love, sex and psychological stimulation; wives were for reproduction, maintaining the household and furnishing dependability. Their individual solutions were admittedly *prudent* in minimising their personal risks and maximising their personal pleasures, but their prudential concerns were rather narrow by modern standards, and they overlooked the moral aspects of intimate relations as presenting occasions for harming others.

Whenever there is a possibility of generating children, or incurring expenses, or displeasing relatives, or having to move house or change jobs, questions of prudence arise that affect the choice of a partner. Adultery raises still other questions of prudence: if discovered, will I lose my house, my fortune, my reputation, a spouse I still like and access to my children? According to divorce lawyers, most people involved in extra-marital affairs have not given these questions much thought until it is too late. An Epicurean will exercise foresight. As Lucretius comments, '[I]t is easier to avoid being lured into the traps of love than, once caught, to extricate yourself from the nets and burst the strong knots of Venus.'

Leaving prudential considerations aside, morality enters the picture whenever deception, manipulation or advantage-taking infects a relationship between two people, and whenever their activities threaten to worsen the lives of others. It might seem odd that, unless you have a communicable disease, you could harm anyone by having sex with them, or just by trying to, any more than you could harm someone by giving them, or just offering them, a cup of tea or a slice of cake. This may be why some men are puzzled when what they thought was a generous offer turns out to constitute sexual harassment. In fact, the cases are rather different, even leaving aside the possibility of an unwanted pregnancy in the tea and cake case.

First, although tea and cake may not be offered entirely unselfishly, any pleasure for the donor requires giving pleasure to the recipient. This is not always true in seduction scenarios. Second, anxious emotions, futile hopes and even pointless expectations can be aroused in the recipient of a sexual offer more readily than in the case of someone offered tea or cake. Third, accepting a cup of tea or a slice of cake need not involve any self-revelation or loss of demeanour that could bring on painful embarrassment. Fourth, you do not insult someone by just offering tea, even if you expect it to be refused, but you can insult them by just offering sex, because many people resent being reduced to attractive bodies.

Adulterous people who behave in a secretive fashion may not realise that they often spread harm that is not imaginary by neglecting their spouse and children and creating confusion and anguish by provoking suspicion. But the Epicurean is not automatically judgemental. The adulterous husband or wife may merely be testing out and enjoying their power over a third party to the latter's detriment, but it is also possible that they are suffering in the confines of marriage. When the starving man steals a pie from the windowsill, he commits an anti-social act that reduces his pain and gives him the intense pleasure of consuming it. He must anticipate punishment, in case he fails to arouse the compassion of the community, and he must decide whether the pie-stealing venture is worth it. By the same token, adulterous lovers must take account of the harm they are causing to others and make an effort to mitigate it. They, too, may be starving, but whether they will attract punishment or compassion is mostly out of their control.

USING YOUR HEAD

The contemporary Epicurean values friendship between men and women and at the same time respects passion. He or she urges us to think carefully about the distinction between nature and convention and the implications it has for human relation-

120

ships and for political decisions. He or she also recognises that relationships pose moral problems, since one or two people's happiness may come at the cost of other people's difficulties and miseries. The Epicurean does not expect either romance or family life to be plain sailing all the way. Love and passion will bring highs and lows, so beware! Don't blame yourself or the other person too harshly. Don't be so judgemental about other people's predicaments. Anguish and uncertainty, the lows as well as the highs, are built into the nature of things.

The Epicurean will be moral as well as prudent. Morality directs us to try to minimise harm to others, even when inflicting such harm has clear prudential advantages for the perpetrator. It is wrong to engineer sex by force, or by offering a quid pro quo to someone who finds you unattractive, as the subsequent experience is bound to be exceedingly unpleasant for them. It is wrong to raise false expectations of permanence in another to obtain sex for a short run. It is wrong to try to control another person's behaviour while enjoying a secret freedom oneself. It is wrong to turn a spouse into a wage slave or a domestic servant.

Epicureans who choose to have children – or who at any rate didn't avoid having children – strive to make the experience as pleasant as possible for themselves as well as for their children. They introduce them to all the sources of pleasure in life: food and drink, gardens, architecture, music, pictures, travel and knowledge. But both mothers and fathers pursue their investigations of the world and their friendships with persons of their own age. They do not sacrifice adult interests and relationships by overzealously arranging and catering to their children's social lives and whims.

By and large, males and females find certain others intriguing and attractive, as the Epicureans insisted, and sometimes irresistibly attractive. The vulnerability to and love for others enables them to form cooperative relationships, to engender and raise children, whether or not they actually do so, and to meet everyday challenges in providing food, shelter, amusement and education to one another and to any offspring. The more they enjoy one another's company and the more willing and able they are to cooperate, the more successful they will be in these endeavours. Nature does, in this sense, care about our happiness. At the same time, conflict is unavoidable. People living in close quarters do not always please one another and, as Lucretius laments, their companionship preferences can change. We have no reason to think that nature has outfitted us with emotions and temperaments that should make our love relations trouble-free as opposed to just good enough for the continuation of the species. Where nature has left us helpless, memories of happier times, prudence with regard to the future, and human agreement have to take over.

8

THINKING ABOUT DEATH

Death ... is nothing to us and does not affect us in the least, now that the nature of the mind is understood to be mortal. [W]hen body and soul, upon whose union our being depends, are divorced, you may be sure that nothing at all will have the power to affect us or awaken sensation in us, who shall not then exist.

Lucretius

Why do you bemoan and beweep death? If your past life has been a boon, and if not all your blessings have flowed straight through you and run to waste like water poured into a riddled vessel ... why, you fool, do you not retire from the feast of life like a satisfied guest?

Lucretius

Trees that have stood for a thousand years are struck by lightning or rot away, and long-lived animals, such as elephants, parrots and tortoises, succumb to accident or disease. Plants decay and become sources of nourishment for other plants, which in turn become sources of nourishment for animals. Mountains erode, seas dry up and galaxies collapse. Everything is reduced to its constituent particles, which nature recombines into new living and lifeless beings.

We are assured that the renewal of life on earth will come to an end. Our sun will burn itself out when its fuel is exhausted in another few billion years, and many physicists believe our entire universe has used up two-thirds of its allotted time and will collapse to its original state in another 5 billion. In the meantime – and it is admittedly a long one – our shoes wear through and our clothes become shabby and useless. Moulds, fungi and bacteria destroy food left sitting too long in order to live and propagate their kind. Moths and termites ruin our clothes and houses.

The individual human being is no exception to the law of limits, what Lucretius calls the 'deep-set boundary posts' of everything except the atoms of nature. The subjective feeling of being an indestructible Self – and some philosophers, including Descartes, seem to have believed they could intuit or prove their own immortality – is an illusion.

How should we then regard the fact that the future is bounded? That there will be no second chance at our own lives, and eventually no human beings? The particles of which we are composed are highly unlikely to regroup themselves after death and to form themselves spontaneously into conscious bodies identical to those of our old selves in our prime, and even if they did, that new person would not be me. If death were only a form of sleep, I might hope to awaken as myself, but the decomposition of the body precludes its being so. The possibility that we can experience paradise after death and be united with our long-lost friends and relatives, or that we will awaken in Hell and be forever deprived of their company, is untenable, along with all its theological variations. There is nothing to hope for and nothing to fear in this regard.

THE EPICUREAN VIEW OF DEATH

The Epicurean position involves three main ideas: death is not to be feared; being dead is not unpleasant or painful; and death is the end – there is no afterlife.

But as well as believing that death was not an evil, Epicurus also believed that being deprived of life is the worst thing that can happen to the individual. This might seem puzzling. Why is it bad to be deprived of life by, for example, being run over by a bus, or through murder, medical negligence or one's own bad habits, if death is not painful and is not to be feared? I'll explore this seeming paradox and then discuss the social implications of the absence of an afterlife.

The fear of death motivates much of our everyday effort and much of our scientific research. We strive to stay alive by watching out for traffic, following the doctor's orders, undergoing surgery and other unpleasant procedures when necessary, and by avoiding dangerous countries or neighbourhoods. When lives are cut short by cancer, or by traffic or sporting accidents, or by rampaging gunmen, it is considered tragic and senseless. Even when life is seriously diminished, though not cut short by old age and the wearing out of the human body's ability to maintain and repair itself, death is regarded as a misfortune, as the worst thing yet that has ever happened to the person who dies. Researchers devote their careers to discovering new cures and better surgical procedures, and the postponement of ageing and the extension of the term of life even by such ghoulish means as suspended animation in freezing storage tanks or blood transfusions, as well as through pills and shots, is increasingly popular. The manipulation of our genes to prolong life is a strategy on the horizon.

It is in one sense rational to fear death and to take steps to avoid dying or being killed. The body is a system of mechanisms for fighting against death: we have an immune system, regulatory systems for dealing with heat and cold, for keeping blood sugar within life-preserving boundaries, for detoxifying and eliminating poisons. Nature has constructed us to derive pleasure from being alive; that is to say, living beings that did not implicitly value their lives and seek to preserve them would not have survived to leave a lineage, given the number and variety of threats to existence that our world contains.

In the prime of life and well beyond it, every animal defends itself against death, struggling to escape from or to counterattack predators, to avoid drowning or suffocating, and humans who are not paralysed with fear, or choosing martyrdom, or suicidal will do the same. Even the very old will sometimes request heroic medical measures to enjoy a few more days, weeks or months of life. We recognise the moral worth of trying to prevent others being killed or dying prematurely, through legislation to reduce massacres and murders by controlling access to weapons and poisons and exposure to environmental toxins, and by regulating machinery such as cars and airplanes. Medical research to cure diseases or prevent physiological conditions that cut people off in infancy, childhood and the prime of life is commendable. How was it possible for the Epicureans to claim that death was not an evil and was not to be feared?

A key idea in Epicureanism is the notion of the 'natural limit'. All household items can be thought of as having a 'best before' date, relative to human interests, and we expect particular items to last that long. This goes not only for eggs and milk, but for cars and vacuum cleaners. The wear and tear of moving parts, chemical deterioration due to heat, oxygen and moisture, and the build-up of dust and minerals cause our electrical and electronic appliances to fail within a specific number of years.

There is usually a period of deterioration before the household object becomes entirely unusable. We can shift this date forwards or backwards to some extent by prudent (refrigeration, mothballs, etc.) or careless and imprudent behaviour, and simple measures can prolong the lives of everyday objects. But there is usually a cost to doing so. The invention of canning dramatically improved the shelf life of fruits, vegetables and meats, but at the cost of flavour and texture. Wood preservatives such as creosote prolong the life of wooden fences, but at a cost to human health through exposure to toxic coal tar derivatives. Life-prolonging drugs have dangerous and unpleasant side effects.

A reasonable person expects food, appliances and clothing to last a certain amount of time and is justifiably annoyed when, despite ordinary levels of prudence, food items spoil, appliances break down and clothes fall apart. The natural limit was not in this case reached, often because of some human failure, or indifference, or even some malicious action, as occasionally happens in factories when unhappy employees seek to punish the employer or consumers by sabotaging the product. Things *should* last, we feel, some definite amount of time.

The Epicurean takes an analogous view of human life. There is a natural limit and a best-before date, though life may still afford sufficient pleasure long after that date has passed. In the natural course of things, we deteriorate and then die because of assaults from other living beings. Bacteria and viruses feed off us, heat and oxygen cause deposits to build up in our organs and blood vessels, and wear and tear affects joints and muscles. Prudent and imprudent actions can shift our expiry dates forward or backward to some degree, but the natural limit remains what it is. No human being has ever been known to live more than 122 years, and very few people, less than 0.1 per cent of the population, are now in their nineties in the UK. Nearly all of them suffer from multiple medical conditions, involving heart, lungs, bones, joints, the brain, skin and other organs; very few remain healthy and active.

Most of us agree that, in theory, 'All men are mortal', but many of us – despite the precautions we take and the sadness we experience over other people's deaths – never manage to internalise the truth that the generalisation applies to me personally. There will come a year that is my last, and then a day that is my last day, not just 'on earth' but anywhere at all. There will be nothing more that the doctors can do, or at least nothing more that I or those who have the authority to make decisions on my behalf will agree to have done for me medically to prolong my life.

This day is not fixed in advance, because how long I will live depends on choices I make regarding diet, habits such as smoking, choice of modes of transportation, driving speeds, participation in dangerous sports, whether to take certain drugs or undergo certain surgeries, and much else. It also depends on chance, or at least on coincidence: for example, whether I happen to be driving over a certain bridge at just the moment it collapses. Nevertheless, this day will come, and as I grow older and older, it will become more and more pointless to blame any particular habit or any intervention for my death. It will not be the doctors' fault that they could not arrest my cancer or replace my failing heart or kidneys in my advanced old age.

Confronting the fact of one's own mortality as well as the decline that is likely to precede it is difficult for most people and it is made more difficult by a culture that tends to regard and report every death as either the dying person or his doctor's moral fault, as a failure to keep hoping and fighting rather than as another instance of the natural limit. When the natural limit is not reached because of accidents, murder or negligence, we look around for someone to blame and seek redress or social adjustments that will reduce the likelihood that someone else is the victim of an accident, murder or negligence. This is rational. What is not rational is blaming the death of a very old person on the doctor's negligence, or her own addiction to ice cream. Even if the deceased was still a lively, engaged and competent person, the wear and tear on the parts of her body invisible to the rest of us were considerable. No one is to blame for her demise.

We imagine being dead to be a terrible experience. There I am, lying in my closed coffin under six feet of earth, my flesh putrefying and being devoured by worms, fungi and bacteria. Or I am being shoved into the oven of the crematorium and then having my bones pulverised.

'When we exist,' Epicurus said, 'death is not yet present, and when death is present, then we do not exist.' If I am dead, I am not having any experiences, good or bad. Those who say of me, 'All her troubles are over', have it right, but those who say of me, 'She is resting peacefully', have it wrong. As long as I am experiencing the good and the bad, I am still alive. If I am resting peacefully, I am definitely still alive.

But shouldn't I fear the process of dying, that it will be excruciatingly painful? Epicurus claimed that as life is evaporating from the body, so is its capacity to sense, feel and think. 'Pains which produce great distress are short in duration; and those which last a long time in the flesh cause only mild distress.'

Is this position consistent with modern medicine or is it just wishful thinking? It is often said that sensory experience, including the sense of pain, diminishes in the last days and hours of life, with hearing the last sense to go, and that the brain and body may be flooded with endorphins as they are under other conditions of severe stress, inducing a sense of peace and contentment. Yet many diseases that lead slowly to death only after months or years or that simply accompany ageing are extremely painful, including cancers, pulmonary conditions and osteoarthritis. Epicurus suffered from multiple health problems, probably including kidney stones, one of the most painful conditions known to medicine. And we have learned, thanks to the work of international medical commissions, what Epicurus seems not to have realised: namely, how widespread health-related suffering really is, with at least 61 million people worldwide affected. A recent article in the British medical journal *The Lancet* estimates that, worldwide, 45 per cent of the dying, the overwhelming majority of them in low- and middle-income settings, experience severe suffering.

Although pain is a fact of life, national legislation directed to insurance, drug prices and palliative care could help many of these people. The importance of adequate pain relief through the use of drugs in later life and at the end of life is understood in theory, but practice lags far behind. Concern about opiate addiction should not be a reason to withhold these merciful and effective compounds.

It might seem that the Epicureans give too little weight to the instinctual fear of death. While denying that death is a kind of sleep, they encourage us to think of it as like sleep, a welcome release from exhaustion and overstimulation or boredom. We can agree that the experiences of a single day can be enjoyable and meaningful even if they are cut off by the need to go to sleep, and even if we can predict approximately when we will succumb to that need. But my virtual certainty that I will awaken to enjoy another day makes the need to go to sleep tonight other than terrifying. And besides, most other people in my locale are asleep as well, so I have no particular 'fear of missing out'. If I believed I would not awaken tomorrow, my pleasure in today would be quickly forgotten. How can we prevent the fear of death from diminishing pleasure in life for us now and overcome the fear of missing out? For someone condemned to die on the scaffold tomorrow, this fear and anger is surely not irrational and is not likely to be removed by philosophy. So how can it be removed for anyone else?

Death at the Right and Wrong Times

When foodstuffs, clothes and appliances do not last as long as they are supposed to we can complain to the manufacturer or vendor, or avoid that product in the future. When babies, young people or old people do not last the amount of time we judge to be appropriate, we cannot complain to the manufacturer, nor can we resolve to avoid that product in the future, so we feel helpless, angry and distraught. We are right to do so, and when our own lives are threatened in mid-life by unexpected diseases we are justified in feeling helpless, angry and distraught. In all such cases, it is appropriate to ask whether anyone is to blame, and whether steps should be taken to reduce this kind of premature death in future. But death occurring around the natural limit of life is not anyone's fault and should not be seen as such. We should instead pay more attention to cases in which not letting someone die, by force feeding or intubating them when they do not wish it, is morally objectionable.

Lucretius recognises that when someone is cut down in the prime of life this is a real misfortune. This person is missing out. 'Never again,' mourners say, 'will your household receive you with joy; never again will the best of wives welcome you home; never again will your dear children race for the prize of your first kisses and touch your heart with pleasure too profound for words.' For ancient people, death at a young age from warfare, shipwreck and infections was a more common occurrence than it is now. For modern people, if you are young and healthy, and take reasonable but not excessive precautions, you should be able to reduce your fear of dying and missing out to a minimum. A prudent person does not join the army voluntarily, or, in Lucretius's view, go to sea. Against fatal fevers and some genetic disorders, however, we are simply helpless. If you are young and have a fatal disease, you will miss out. Nature has indeed dealt you a very bad hand, singling you out as it were. You are entitled to mourn your fate and to express your feelings of radical injustice.

For the very old who 'bewail and bemoan the approach of death to an immoderate degree', however, Lucretius has no sympathy at all. Nature, if she could speak, he says, would be justified in addressing them harshly: 'Stop snivelling, you dolt ... You had full use of all the precious things of life before you reached this senile state ... Because you continually crave what is not present and scorn what is, your life has slipped away from you incomplete and unenjoyed ... Quick then, discard all behaviour unsuited to your age and with equanimity yield to your years; for yield you must.'

This may seem harsh. Even the very old are entitled to their regret that they will be missing out. They will not see their great-grandchildren grow up, or experience the return of Halley's comet, or enjoy 100 more ice-cream cones or bridge games. They won't find out who the next president is going to be, or the one after that, or whether there is life on Mars, and they will never be able to find out much more that they would like to find out. These cravings are not unseemly; nor does it seem in the least unbecoming for old people to express these regrets, which are, after all, an affirmation of life and its pleasures and their love for other people. But these regrets about missing out should be expressed with calm and dignity. If you are old, accept the inevitable. Try to minimise problems for your descendants by leaving your financial affairs in good order and not adding confusion to the grief they are likely to feel after you are gone. Their grief, the grief of the living, is anything but irrational. A source of pleasure, your presence, your conservations, your help and friendship has really been taken away from them.

Many people do not want to think about death or plan for it by discussing their eventual demise with their relatives, by ensuring that their wills are up to date and reflect their wishes, and by writing out clear instructions for how they wish their last months, days and hours to go. Yet those who do take these measures are far less anxious at the end of life than those who avoid the whole subject. The thought that I will not live to see my children reach the age I am now saddens me, but that is all the more reason to talk to them now about their hopes and expectations for the future and to communicate my love for them. In advanced old age, many try to reconnect with long-lost friends, repair broken friendships and forgive old enemies, which brings a kind of peace.

The Epicurean position is that it's bad to have your life taken away from you by others, or by yourself, or by external causes when you have not reached the natural limit set by the normal human body. The fact that *it's* natural death cannot be bad *for* the individual and that dying need not be painful doesn't imply that it will be good under all circumstances. As observed, when a child dies of leukaemia or a middle-aged woman of breast cancer, or an elderly man still on his feet is run over by a bus, this is unfortunate; just as it is unfortunate to be shot or stabbed to death.

Abortion vs Infanticide

If it isn't bad to be dead, and if we can accept death as in some ways a good thing that makes space in the world for vigorous new life, what's wrong with murder and capital punishment? Or, for that matter, infanticide? And if dying needn't be painful, why should suicide by the despondent necessarily be discouraged?

Many people are troubled by abortion, which they view as murder, and as no different in principle from infanticide. In both cases, a life is struggling to exist – in one case it is still a foetus dependent on its mother's circulatory system for oxygen and nourishment; in the other case it has been born, breathes air and drinks milk, but why, they ask, should this make a difference?

In both cases, it seems, we put an end to a life that in the normal course of events would have been lived for the usual length of time, and that could have been happy, or at least a mixture of happy and unhappy. In both cases, we might be reducing someone's troubles in caring for a baby or a child. So why should abortion and infanticide be regarded differently? Shouldn't both be permitted or both prohibited?

Here are two common arguments that will not carry any weight with an Epicurean:

- Undergoing pregnancy and the responsibility of caring for a child under adverse circumstances are just punishments for having sex outside of marriage. Denial of abortion to women will produce more responsible behaviour.
- A woman has a right to decide what to do with her own body. The foetus is part of her body before it is born, so a woman has a right to decide to abort a foetus or not.

Epicureans do not regard sex outside of marriage as a crime deserving punishment, so the issue of deterrence is irrelevant. They do regard it as immoral to impose serious burdens and difficulties, such as those involved in bearing and raising children, on people who do not want them or not so soon. But

Epicureans also regard rights as conventional and culture-relative. The right to one's own body and its contents cannot exist before the decision to recognise it has been taken, and that recognition is precisely what is in question.

Because law, when it is based on moral concern, has the function of preventing harm to individuals, according to the Epicurean, the case for abortion and against infanticide can only concern the balance of harm and help that is caused by permitting or forbidding abortion versus the degree of harm and help caused by permitting or forbidding infanticide in the culture under discussion.

Permitting abortion prevents certain grave harms. These include the impoverishment of parents who cannot afford to raise a child; the neglect of infants and children by parents who must work to survive and who have no help; and the abuse of unwanted infants and children. It also prevents the harms of illegal abortion, physical injury, infection and sometimes death. Although not all women who abort are preventing grave suffering to themselves or their offspring, and although some are doubtless depriving themselves of the pleasures having a child would have brought them, the costs of an anti-abortion policy are far greater than the benefits of making it obligatory to try to bring new life into the world whenever conception occurs. Only someone like the Christian saint Augustine, who said, 'I fail to see what use woman can be to man, if one excludes the function of bearing children', could entirely disregard the plans women have for themselves that do not include having a child within nine months from now.

Although the Epicureans did not work out (as far as we know) a position on abortion and infanticide, I would reconstruct the Epicurean position on the difference between them as follows: permitting infanticide or the killing of young children could prevent some of the same harms as abortion, such as poverty, neglect and abuse. But the infant, unlike the foetus, is a member of human society even before its sensory apparatus is working well and before it can speak. Even if it is unwanted by its parents, it makes its needs evident, and these needs can be satisfied, and can only be satisfied by human attention and effort directed towards it. The morally right thing to do is to meet the needs of an unwanted child through adoption or foster care. The foetus is not a member of human society, even though abortion injures it and puts an end to its life. No form of foster care for a foetus is conceivable, not even by hardened foes of abortion. A policy against infanticide spares the life of many children who would otherwise be in danger of death, despite belonging to human society; a policy against abortion does not.

SUICIDE VS EUTHANASIA

Suicide presents another difficult problem. If pain is the only true evil, and if death is not painful or an evil, it might seem that if you are in severe mental or physical pain, there is an easy way to be free of it. Just kill yourself in some painless or at least low-pain way. The Stoics recommended suicide for all sorts of reasons, including political disgrace, getting old and frail, and being tired of life.

The Epicurean objection to this argument is that suicide is usually both imprudent and immoral. 'It is absurd to pursue death because you are weary of life,' Epicurus is reported as saying, 'when you have made death worth pursuing by your way of life.' Although Lucretius's own suicide at the age of about forty-five belies Epicurus's own thinking, it is significant that his act was performed, according to ancient testimony, under the influence of a poisonous drug.

Suicide is almost always based on the misperception of actual circumstances, and a failure to appreciate the courses of action that can remove suffering. It is overwhelmingly likely that the suffering of the despondent person, though its badness now is not in question, will not be as long lasting as he or she thinks. To kill yourself for love in the belief that the unattainable object was uniquely perfect for you shows you to be in the grip of a delusion. Because political office, wealth and influence depend on convention and are unnatural and unnecessary, it is absurd to sacrifice life itself when they are lost.

Even blindness, Epicurus thought, is bearable. His view is borne out by studies that show that most people adjust to conditions that to an active and healthy person sound unbearable, such as becoming quadriplegic. They come to terms with their condition within twelve months or so and begin once more to take pleasure in what life has to offer. The ability to regain equilibrium may be hard pressed during an illness when we feel terrible, but it tends to work until we reach the natural limit of life. In the same way, the mind can deal with frustration and grief by making it possible to forget and by enabling us to remember happier times and to look forward to their return.

Further, suicide usually harms others severely and so is usually immoral. It is cruel to the parents or children or friends of the suicide, who may be haunted for the rest of their lives. It may be intended to punish others for their neglect or treachery, but it is more punishment than could fit any such crime and is unlikely to have an improving influence.

But let's take a hard case. You are in intractable physical pain; every breath is an agony and there is nothing the doctors can do. Your friends and family are tormented by your suffering and there is nothing they can do, either. Or you have reached a great age, none of your friends are still living, your children have no interest in you; you have multiple illnesses, and you are losing the ability to see, hear, taste and remember, and all means of enjoyment are gone. Should you end your life to end these dreadful conditions? There is no question of your right to die for the Epicurean, but it is arguably imprudent for you to continue to live. You commit no moral injury if you ingest too many of your sleeping pills or enlist the help of a sympathetic doctor.

Resisting and Accepting Mortality

Many scientists are hopeful of discovering the keys to the regeneration of our worn-out organs, to the substitution of robust artificial organs for our flesh and blood versions, and to gene therapies that might make us immortal. While the prevention of pain and the remediation of disability through medicine is an aim the Epicurean will warmly endorse, the achievement of immortality through technology is not.

You might reasonably wish to live to, say, ninety-five in a state of poor health as opposed to living only to the age of eighty-five in fairly good health, but the indefinite prolongation of life, as some futurists dream of it, is a short-sighted goal. It is imprudent to wish to live so long that you outlive your friends and your children and others of your generation, even if you can do so in a state of robust health, thanks to gene manipulation and new drugs. There will be no one with whom you can share your and their first-person memories of the past. Watching your children die after you have watched your parents die will be agonising for you. Will being able to follow politics and culture into the 22nd century, to see more new movies and to enjoy more meals and walks, really compensate for the loss of those you loved? Perhaps your friends and children – and their friends and their children – will also live long? The need for food, water and living space rules out the possibility that everybody can live indefinitely, unless we colonise new planets where we'll probably have to live under glass domes breathing artificial air, and when you've lived long enough you'll have lost track of who your descendants are and where they are.

The perspective that comes with accepting mortality at the natural limit has important consequences. We need to remember that our minds as well as our bodies are under constant assault from living entities – viruses, fungi and bacteria, struggling to exist at our expense. We are attacked as well from minute toxic particles and complexes of particles in air, water and foodstuffs that have no parasitic intentions but happen to be disruptive in the body, like the metallic particles emitted from vehicle exhausts, or the fructose molecule, or the aldehydes created by the metabolism of alcohol. Suffering and death can arrive much too soon, not only on account of individual decisions, but because of political decisions and the absence of political will. It is important to understand the role of these tiny entities, the by-products of civilisation. We use antibiotics and antivirals; we try to filter out arsenic and benzene in drinking water and particulates in the air, and to limit exposure to X-rays and elec-tromagnetic radiation. When people do not fear and do not take steps to prevent damage caused by these minute entities, when it is easy to do so, they fail to prevent needless suffering and premature death.

The environment cannot be made perfectly safe. But – since this biological life is the only one any of us is ever going to have – we should welcome legislation that recognises the role of these subvisible entities even when, as with new controls on diesel emissions or tobacco, or a price rise on sugary drinks, or the banning of poisonous food additives and colourants, it is inconvenient. The difference of a few years of health or life, especially life in the absence of pain, is unimportant in the history of the universe. But to me, from the first-person standpoint, and to those close to me from their standpoints, even a small postponement is meaningful.

The other side of Lucretius's withering scorn for the elderly complainant who finds life too short is his urging not to postpone enjoyments, either when you are young or when you are old. When you are young, remember that some day you may be too old and frail to take long trips to far away destinations, to eat nuts and raw carrots, and to stay up late binge-watching box sets. Do these enjoyable things while you still can. Then, when you are old, realise that the sacrifices one would recommend to a young person in the name of prudence no longer apply to you. If you want to eat a tub of ice cream every day or smoke cigarettes at the age of eighty-five, no one should interfere with you on the grounds that these pleasures will shorten your life.

Accepting mortality as implying the end of all choosing, avoiding and experiencing while valuing life is a conceptual balancing act, but not an impossible one. From the cosmological perspective of Epicureanism, the integrity of mind and body is a wonderful phenomenon. The absorption of particles through respiration and nutrition, their loss through excretion and abrasion, the processes of repair and those of deterioration occur within a body that looks much the same from day to day, as long as it meets with no violent accident, and within a mind that feels from the inside much the same from day to day. But a person is a temporary entity like every other; robust from a short-term perspective, but fragile from a long-term perspective. My dying liberates the particles from which I am composed to form more vigorous entities. I make room for new people to have the experience of childhood, of discovery, growth and learning, that they could not have if people like me were to live indefinitely long lives. I sacrifice my hunger for experience, knowledge and sensation; I would have liked more, but what I have had will be sufficient when the time comes. In the meantime, I must cultivate friendships, make amends and enjoy the days and hours left to me.

Don't Count on the Afterlife

'What of Cerberus,' Lucretius asks, invoking the three-headed dog who guarded the gates of Hell in ancient mythology, 'and the Furies, and the realm destitute of life? These terrors do not exist and cannot exist anywhere at all.' One reason for the widespread belief in the immortality of the soul and the existence of an afterlife is that human beings have a strong sense of justice and desert. We tend to believe firmly that harms done to other people deserve punishment and that superhuman forces will ensure punishment when human forces fail to do so. We suppose that, thanks to these powerful forces, 'what goes around comes around.'

Most of the world's religions teach explicitly that wrongdoing will always be punished and patient suffering and endurance rewarded. They instruct believers that all undeserved misery will be compensated for by happiness or even bliss, and that all unjust profit and pleasure enjoyed by the wicked in their lifetimes will be paid for many times over by their torments. If this does not happen in the course of the individual's life, it must happen in the life or lives we will all awaken to after death, reincarnated as animals, or babies, or angels, or inhabitants of Heaven or Hell. Injustice is thus seen as only a temporary condition that has to be put up with for the time being. Conversely, it seems that if human beings are truly mortal, there is no certainty that justice will be done. Unless people believe they cannot get away with their crimes indefinitely, they will give free rein to their worst appetites.

Epicurean ethics, as Chapter 6 (pages 95–108) showed, regards society as reasonably effective in maintaining considerate and virtuous behaviour, thanks to our possession of a guilt-inducing conscience and through the punishment of humans by humans. At the same time, the Epicurean recognises that it is possible to get away with harms to others and that some people are never troubled by conscience because they lack it. There are assaults, murders and rapes that are never punished because the perpetrator is never identified. There are kidnappings, bank robberies and art heists that are a total success from the criminal point of view. Other people can hurt our feelings, ruin our job prospects and steal our mates, and never suffer from guilt or social ostracism. Warmongers have caused the death, maiming and displacement of millions and lived to happy and ripe old ages. And the rich can exploit the poor economically and keep them in a state of deprivation by controlling politics and the law, again without experiencing the slightest remorse.

People who know or believe themselves to be especially clever and powerful do not fear public exposure and punishment. Psychopaths who derive pleasure from manipulating and tormenting their victims do not suffer from regret and guilt. Their assumption that they are unlikely to be caught and punished may be erroneous, but Epicurean considerations are unable to deter them and may even encourage them if they know they have nothing to fear from the oversight of God or the gods.

The Epicurean has to accept the implication that there is no assurance justice will be done in the long-run. No cosmic process ensures this, and hope for or fear of an afterlife cannot provide sound reasons for living an orderly and innocent life and desisting from crime. Our commitment to morality must rest on a preference for compassion, respect and fairness, and be backed up by a desire for approval, internalised as self-approval, and a fear of others and the pain of a bad conscience.

Justice for the individual has to be secured, if it is to be secured at all, in his or her lifetime, preferably when it still matters, and justice for groups of people has to be secured within the lifetime of the group. The great social movements of the 19th and 20th centuries, including the reforms introduced into prisons and workhouses, the abolition of American slavery and the introduction of labour legislation, were stimulated by the recognition that this life matters because it is the only life any of us will ever have. The expectation that the sufferings of the meek and poor would be amply repaid in Heaven, provided they obeyed priests and rulers, and that the predatory and brutal would receive their just deserts in Hell was no longer sufficiently powerful to justify complacency. Social justice, the reformers realised, was up to human beings themselves, and in particular to those most committed to compassion, respect and fairness.

PART III

SEEKING KNOWLEDGE AND AVOIDING ERROR

9

WHAT IS REAL?

A property is what cannot under any circumstances be severed and separated from a body ... such is the relationship of heaviness to rocks, heat to fire, liquidity to water ... On the other hand, to slavery, poverty and wealth, freedom, war, concord, and all other things whose coming and going does not impair the essential nature of a thing, we ... apply the appropriate term accidents.

Lucretius

All events without exception have, unlike matter, no independent existence.

Lucretius

NATURE AND CONVENTION

In the passage above, Lucretius draws a distinction between, on the one hand, the heaviness of rocks and the heat of fire, and on the other the poverty of a person or the concord existing between two nations. He implies that heat and weight belong more intrinsically and enduringly to some things than poverty and concord do to others.

The topic of 'essential natures' is important because many errors of judgement arise from confusing 'accidental' properties with 'essential' properties and from confusing the conventional with the natural. Poverty, for example, is not an irremediable property of many of the residents of our inner cities, though it can appear that way. Belligerence is likely to characterise foreign nations only as long as they feel threatened or harbour fantasies of domination. Masculinity and femininity, though they have a biological basis, are associated by purely cultural conventions with distinct and exaggerated forms of dress, speech, occupation and behaviour. How we react to 'poverty', 'belligerence' and 'masculinity' is for the most part conditioned by our diverse educations, exposure to different media, our own limited experience and the workings of our ever-active imaginations.

To take a step backwards before pursuing this line of thought, if all that really exists are atoms and void, what should we think about the middle-sized objects that surround us, and about our own bodies? Aren't they all, along with people and nations, things that come and go, accidental things that are illusions of a sort? Optically blurred combinations of something like atoms and void?

Some philosophical traditions, notably those originating in India, where atomism is also believed to have started before spreading to Greece, do hold that the world of experience is an illusion. But how would the sun or the fire warm us if it were merely illusory? Why take an aspirin to cure a headache if the headache is illusory and the aspirin tablets, too, are visual illusions? If objects, people and landscapes were illusions, created by our illusory brains, it would be unsound to regard the senses as the basis of our knowledge.

Implicitly, the Epicurean distinguishes between three levels of reality: the eternal, indestructible things – the atoms; natural composites of atoms like animals, plants, geological formations, sun, moon, stars; and conventional things – driving licences, royalty, clocks, chess games.

Natural things are active. They have causal powers, arising from their invisible constitutions. Humans and other animals can act on their environments by eating, building shelters and moving things around. Plants have nourishing and poisonous properties. Other non-living things have powers as well. Large rocks present obstacles to some crawling and climbing animals but serve as good habitats for others. The stars illuminate the night sky. Even if all humans were to fall victim to a virus that affected only our species but affected it rapidly and fatally, other natural things would continue to exist and to exercise their causal powers on other natural things.

Conventional things, though we come across them all the time in everyday experience, seem to belong to a different category from the natural things. They have no causal powers of their own. They depend for their existence on human agreement and on human cooperative efforts. We *make* them and use them. They serve specifically human needs and interests, and these interests change frequently. When they do, we may lose interest in making them, using them and caring for or about them. Examples of conventional things include clocks, money, driving licences, aristocrats and chessboards.

If our species were wiped out by a virus, I can imagine that there would still be driving licences and bills in our wallets, dead royals, clocks that would eventually stop ticking and chessboards and chess pieces in drawers and closets. But if our species had never existed in the first place, none of these things would exist. I can imagine physical objects looking exactly like today's pound coins or exactly like cuckoo clocks, forming by chance in a world without humans. I can even form a mental image of a group of dinosaurs peering curiously at a clock, but I can also form a mental image of a group of dinosaurs peering curiously at Queen Victoria. It does not follow that Queen Victoria could have existed in the era of the dinosaurs. If an object looking exactly like one of today's pound coins had by chance self-assembled in ancient Assyria, it would not have been a pound coin.

For money to function as money, people have to believe it is not just paper with a picture and numbers on it. They have to believe it is worth getting hold of, and easy to exchange for other things. Royals, aristocrats and commoners exist only because, as a society, we believe them to exist. We made up some rules that specify who is an aristocrat of what sort, just as we made up the rules for chess. The hereditary aristocrat and the royals play the game of being special people called viscounts, princesses and marquises, and many of us play along with them.

You might object that money, driving licences and chess have causal effects on the world and so are really no different from natural things. Money allegedly makes the world go round. Driving licences make teenagers sign up for driving lessons. Chess causes obsessions in some people and gives rise to lucra-tive competitions. But money all by itself can't actually cause cash registers to display numbers, foodstuffs to flow into my household and grocery magnates to feel joy or dismay. The causes of these interrelated phenomena are the beliefs of the people who seek and use money; beliefs that depend on others around them sharing the same beliefs: that money is desirable, that it can be exchanged for goods and services, and that you can't make it yourself, and have to earn it from someone who has it and who wants something from you. It wasn't Princess Margaret's *being* an aristocrat that caused her to behave in an arrogant fashion or that prevented her intended marriage to the commoner Peter Townsend. The cause of her behaving in an arrogant fashion was some kind of neurological configuration together with her experiences of life, and it was the actions of the powerful people around her that prevented her marriage.

THINGS IN BETWEEN

You might object that the distinction between the natural and the conventional is not sharp, and you would be right. Although humans have never created a new species, they have created hybrid animals and breeds of dog, sheep and cattle, as well as many fruits that would not have existed in nature otherwise. They exist only because of human interests and efforts. But they have the same causal powers as wild animals and fruits, and it seems strange to say that dachshunds and plums exist only by convention on the grounds that if there had been no humans there would not have been dachshunds or plums. War, to use Lucretius's example of something not quite as real as heat, is defined by jurists. Poverty is defined by bureaucrats. Neither one is a category a biologist would recognise. In this sense, war and poverty exist 'by convention'. But try telling a poor person trying to collect change for a meal or someone in the midst of a battle about this philosophical discovery. Poverty and war have actual effects.

Many other things are hard to categorise. Take the notion of a pesticide. From one perspective, pesticides are entirely natural. There are toxic chemicals found in roots, leaves and seeds that belong to the defence systems of wild plants. They function to prevent the plants' lives or reproduction being shortened or elim-inated by insects, birds and mammals. Some of these naturally occurring chemicals, such as those found in chrysanthemums and citronella, are used by humans.

From another perspective, the very idea of a pesticide depends on human conceptions of the hurtful and the beneficial, and most pesticides are synthetic, manufactured chemical compounds that cannot be found in nature. Agriculture-practising human beings, who emerged in around the 10th century BCE, developed the concept of a nuisance insect and thereafter experimented with smokes and poisons applied to their crops to kill them. The word 'pesticide', however, didn't come into our language until 1939. Further, the understanding of the term has altered dramatically since the 1990s because we care about different things than formerly and see the world in different ways. Pesticides were formerly understood in our culture as beneficial synthetic chemicals that promoted better living, providing food and profits to hundreds of millions. Today pesticides are widely understood as poisons churned out by cynical conglomerates that kill indiscriminately, destroy long-established ecological balances and have detrimental effects on human health.

Could there be pesticides in a world without human beings? Some leftover cans of Raid might remain in a world from which all human beings had been eradicated, and objects looking exactly like cans of Raid might spontaneously form in a world without human beings, but they would be like the useless pound coins left over after the universal plague.

If there were no human beings to make decisions, to create new substances and animals, and to invent terminology, there would be no wars, no poverty, no dachshunds, aristocrats or pesticides in the sense that most of us use those terms. But then nothing would ever be identified as 'an atom' or 'an elementary particle' in the sense in which we use those terms, because there would be no one around to do science. There would be no rules laid down in the form of definitions for what constitutes 'an elementary particle'. Still, atoms, quarks, gluons, bosons, etc., would continue to act and so to exist.

It is accordingly impossible to draw a sharp line between 'things whose existence depends on our needs, interests, decisions and inventions' and 'things with independent existence'. Nevertheless, to think like an Epicurean is to be aware of how very different social reality is from natural reality. Social reality contains laws thought up by humans, and with them, trials, prisons and prison sentences, practices such as cattle farming and factory labour, and institutions such as universities, senates and film studios. These elements of social reality exist only in virtue of our beliefs about their importance and usefulness, and our cooperation in keeping them going. Any of them could disappear a century from now. Nevertheless, social reality has a profound effect on nature through our laws, practices and institutions. We change nature at a much faster rate than nature would change herself. And this raises ethical problems of which the Epicureans themselves were unaware, but with which the Epicurean of right now must be concerned.

HUMAN RIGHTS: NATURAL OR CONVENTIONAL?

In 1948, the UN passed a groundbreaking resolution recognising thirty human rights, including the right to equality, to desirable work, to social security, to rest and leisure, to be free of slavery and torture, and to be able to move freely out of one's country.

Rights are often called 'natural'. The suggestion is that, like the heat of fire and the heaviness of rocks, they belong intrinsically to human beings rather than being 'accidents' that can come and go, like poverty or concord. We suppose that even if some people, as a matter of fact, lack provisions for social security or cannot leave their countries, they nevertheless have the right to do so, a right that is not being acknowledged by those in charge. But did politicians discover by somehow peering into the human interior that these rights pertained naturally to human beings, though they had not all been recognised before? Or was the UN asserting a list of new conventions that they deemed ought to be respected, whether they are or not, by its member states?

The ancient Stoics, who first used the concept of a natural right, derived the notion of a right of self-defence from the observation that all animals try to remain alive and to defend themselves. Seeing this tendency in nature, they denied that the right to self-preservation was merely conventional. It had to be supported and enforced by human law, but the right, they thought, existed before the laws designed to uphold it. The notion of a right to life rooted in nature is today applied to matters as varied as abortion, capital punishment, warfare, euthanasia and healthcare. Belief in a right to life can motivate the bombing of abortion clinics, as well as the refusal of the pacifist to take part in any form of human-versus-human violence. It can motivate protests and efforts to legislate against capital punishment or physician-assisted suicide, and for free healthcare.

Jeremy Bentham, a 19th-century Epicurean philosopher, famously described rights as 'nonsense on stilts'. As the Epicurean sees matters, rights exist only by convention and are not found in nature. Legally sanctioned rights that to our eyes look obviously conventional, such as the right an 18th-century nobleman had to beat his servants, looked far more natural to our ancestors, and Bentham was sensitive to just this kind of abuse.

For the Epicurean, where self-preservation is concerned, there is only broad human agreement that we *may* with impunity take measures to preserve our own lives, even if these measures harm or inconvenience others. We can regard the UN as setting out a reasoned agenda as to what the minimum standards for a decent human life are, and what it is the responsibility of human institutions to try to ensure. But rights are causally powerless and can't make anything happen. Only human decisions to 'stick up for one's rights', to insist on or enforce a right legally can make things happen. That is why many of the rights listed by the UN are consistently violated by member states, such as the ban on torture and slavery.

Because rights are made by agreement, not discovered in nature, they are subjects of disagreement. It is no wonder that people argue over the rights of the unborn, the rights of animals and the right to bear arms. If these things existed in nature, we would have discovered them by observation. But that is not how they got into the arena of discussion. The right to life can be enshrined in law or customary practice as a convention, but it's up to us to decide in what cases we want to invoke that right and enforce compliance and in what cases we want to deny that it applies. The anti-militarist and the anti-abortion advocate are likely to find themselves on different sides, though both cite the right to life as the basis for their positions. Such alleged rights as the right to free speech or the right to bear arms are equally conventional rather than natural and accordingly poorly defined. Again, it is up to us to decide how to interpret the right to either one, what specifically to allow in its name, and what specifically to prohibit.

The Imaginary: Unthings

A fourth category, in addition to atoms, natural things and conventional things, implicit in Epicurean theory is that of the imaginary. Imaginary things are believed to belong to nature and are explicitly ascribed potent causal powers. According to our best theories, however, they do not exist.

Here are some examples of Unthings: ghosts, angels, unicorns, sorcery, phlogiston, lucky numbers.

Belief in ghosts is remarkably prevalent and exists across all cultures. People all over the world believe that the spirits of the dead roam the earth and visit the living to terrify, warn or advise them. They pay money to mediums to get in touch with the departed. Narratives by people who have seen a ghost and, more recently, photographs of ghosts taken with phones, abound on the Internet. Although ghosts are considered highly active, and even as possessing supernatural powers, such as being able to travel through walls, they do not behave like other persons in having addresses, needing food, bearing children and so on.

Do ghosts exist? The answer is yes, of course! – if what this means is that we all know what a ghost is, that most cultures have a word for 'ghost' in their native language and that most people can recite the qualities belonging to ghosts in their cultural tradition. In ours, ghosts are semi-transparent, whitish and appear and disappear suddenly. In other traditions they look exactly like regular people or assume the form of foxes. Unicorns, sorcery and lucky numbers exist in the same sense as ghosts do, and so does phlogiston, a fiery substance 18th-century chemists supposed to be liberated from flammable materials when they were ignited. All the Greek and Roman gods exist, too, in the sense under discussion. People can be convinced that they are affected by witchcraft or watched over by angels, so, in a sense, witchcraft and angels exist.

Yet we do remove items from the category of the real when we make certain discoveries about the world and the causes of our experiences. We discover that phenomena we supposed were caused in one way can actually be explained in some other way. The lonely sailors who seemingly spotted mermaids on distant rocks were looking at sea mammals unrelated to women. Mermaids are Unthings.

Lucretius helpfully promises to explain what 'gives us the terrifying illusion of hearing and seeing face to face people who are dead, and whose bones are embosomed in the earth'. The air, he says, is full of images, some of them formed spontaneously from stray atoms given off from actual bodies. Some of them enter our heads when we are asleep, causing dreams, others when we are awake, causing hallucinations. The images are actually 'membranes stripped from the surfaces of objects [that] float this way and that through the air. It is these that visit us when we are awake or asleep and terrify our minds each time we see weird forms and phantoms.' This is not exactly how we explain the ubiquity of belief in ghosts today, and you might think it makes ghosts all too material, but the point is clear. The dead have no existence in the world of the living, except as ideas and images. Ghosts are images that do not have causal powers over anything except the human mind.

The category of 'things we have learned are not real' is important for a number of reasons. First, belief in Unthings leads to futile and harmful actions and blocks useful discoveries. Chemistry could not make further progress until phlogiston was discarded in favour of a better theory of combustion. Relying on lucky and unlucky numbers can lead to bad decisions at the gaming table or in real-estate purchases. It might be hard to think of disadvantages resulting from believing in angels, but if you don't count on your guardian angel to save you, you may avoid some disasters.

Even more important, fear and contempt are emotions that attach to Unthings. Fear and anxiety can be alleviated by discovering that ghosts and sorcery do not exist. People have died of fright when they believed themselves to be haunted. Finding out that sorcery does not work could save you from the anguished belief that you are a sorcerer's doomed victim lying under a curse.

Many other Unthings give rise to fear or contempt, including 'the Jewish conspiracy to control the world' and 'racial inferiority'. These Unthings are supposed by those who believe them to be real to be powerful causes of what we observe in the world.

Racial and ethnic inferiority is seen by some people as the cause of the poverty and degradation of the people regarded as belonging to inferior races and ethnicities. It is supposed to be a natural condition, and many scientists, reputable in their own day, provided testimony (unreliable testimony) as to the reality of superior and inferior races.

Supposedly, you can see with your own eyes how racial inferiority exerts its powerful effects. Victorian writers compared village life in Africa or among the 'naked savages' of South America with life in their well-upholstered drawing rooms with newspapers and gas lamps. The 'natives' had seemingly failed to invent firearms and steam engines and had not advanced to the higher moral state of wearing head-to-foot body-disguising clothing. This state of affairs seemed to the Victorians plainly to indicate superior intelligence, drive and ethics on the part of the English, and dim-wittedness, laziness and excessive sensuality on the part of the others. Until anthropology and history came to be written in new ways, it was difficult to grasp that the pathways taken by different populations from the 1st millennia BCE to near the end of the 2nd century CE were different, involving both chance – the 'swerve' – and choice, and that intrinsic inferiority and superiority had nothing to do with it.

Today, a similar inference to the Victorian one tempts many people. They observe urban neighbourhoods occupied predominantly by people with darker skin who appear poor and idle, and, by contrast, neighbourhoods occupied predominantly by people with light skin who appear busy and prosperous. Their eyes are not deceiving them. Many careful sociological studies will confirm that their perceptions are accurate. The rate of poverty among black Americans is more than double the rate of poverty among white Americans, and the unemployment rate is almost double as well. It is easy to see why the inference to intrinsic inferiority and superiority gets made, insofar as the actual causes of the observed phenomena are equally invisible to direct perception. But racial inferiority, considered as a causal factor whose effect is poverty and crime, is as much an Unthing as is racial superiority, considered as a causal factor whose workings explain wealth and law-abidingness. This can be seen from the dismal effects of the policy changes of the last twenty years. The widespread view that, because the poor are intrinsically lazy, motivating men and women to seek work in the private sector by withholding welfare payments would cure poverty proved to be a delusion. You can see with your own eyes that this did not work by taking a walk in certain parts of East London or the South Bronx of New York. Human beings have not changed in their intrinsic talents and motivations over the past two decades; what has failed to improve or has worsened are the policies governing housing, zoning, development in the cities and suburbs, and welfare payments.

As a belief in ghosts can have powerful effects on the human mind, the belief in inferior and superior races, and people's own beliefs that they belong to one or the other, can have powerful causal workings. These beliefs are formed by and then work together with laws and customs that create and maintain poverty, including, in the US, zoning laws, the custom of funding schools by property taxes, the custom of imposing fees for medical care and childcare, and habitual practices by real-estate agents. None of this has anything to do with intrinsic natures. False belief and bad practice together are adequate to explain the difference between the prosperous and busy community and the poor and idle community.

Just as pernicious as the view that words and phrases in circulation always refer to something that really exists and has causal powers independent of human beliefs and preferences is the view that only what we can see with our own eyes is real and causally efficacious. People fear dying in a plane crash or as a result of a terrorist attack because they observe these events on TV and trust, as they should, the reports of reliable witnesses about them. Such things really happen and they make a vivid visual and auditory impression. But they are very rare. The chances of being killed in such a disaster are far lower than the chances of being killed in an ordinary automobile accident. People do not fear, as much as it would be prudent to, invisible forms of radiation in dental X-rays, or electromagnetic radiation given off by household appliances and cell phones, or the atoms of toxic chemicals in plastics or pesticides or cigarettes. Don't suppose that what you can't see or otherwise sense must be a causally inefficacious Unthing.

But couldn't it sometimes at least be a good idea, you might wonder, to ignore the powers of causally potent invisible things and, correspondingly, to believe in causally powerful Unthings? There is a lot of stress involved in trying to defend oneself against X-rays, microwaves, benzene molecules in our drinking water, parasites and bacteria in our foodstuffs, and harmful particles in the exhaust of trucks and cars. Conversely, putting one's trust in Unthings, such as the healing power of crystals or good-luck socks, might be soothing and strengthening. Maybe so, but the Epicurean will be alert to the difference between the real causal powers of invisible things and the actual powerlessness of things whose effects, if any, are really just the effects of her own mind.

THE REALITY OF THE PAST

What sense can be made of Lucretius's remark that events have no independent existence? 'When people assert that the rape of Helen and the subjugation of the people of Troy are facts,' he cautions, 'beware of possibly being trapped by them into an acknowledgement that these events have an independent existence simply because those generations of human beings, of whom they were accidents, have been swept away beyond recall.' If there had been no material substance, no atoms, Lucretius says, 'the beauty of Tyndareus's daughter [Helen of Troy] would never have fanned into flame the passion smouldering deep in Paris's heart'.

This seems a strange argument on the face of it. Surely the fact that had there never been matter or people, the Trojan War would not have existed, doesn't mean that it didn't happen. There is material substance, after all, and isn't the world the determinate way it is because of the arrangements and activities of its underlying elements? Isn't there also a determinate way it was in the past because of the arrangements and activities of its underlying elements as they were? Can anyone deny that the Holocaust, the Cambodian and Armenian genocides, along with some version of the Trojan War, actually happened?

Although we can no longer point to Helen or Achilles, and all the rest of the participants in the Trojan War, as the bearers of actions and experiences, surely some testimony that is handed down from generation to generation is reliable, even if not all of it is?

The key term is 'independent existence'. Lucretius (who appears to take the Helen story more seriously than modern scholars) is not denying that the Trojan War happened in the same way that a modern Holocaust denier would deny that the Holocaust happened, or some conspiracy theorists deny that humans ever landed on the moon. His point could be expressed as follows. The fact that there was a Holocaust has a 'dependent' existence. From the perspective of the universe, the atoms were reshuffled into new combinations. From our human perspective, an event of momentous significance took place, one which matters to us because of the suffering that took place, and because we still find it difficult to understand how the torture and persecution of human by human on such a scale can come about. Human evaluations, as well as human language and experience, are required for there to be facts at all, and this applies to the present as well as to the past.

Further, historical events have to be reconstructed from people's eyewitness reports, the records and lists they decide to keep, and their memoirs. These have to be pieced together and reconciled to make up a historical narrative. Historians strive to be objective. They work from their written and oral data, trying to weed out propaganda, prejudice and sheer invention. We read history books with the aim of finding out what actually happened, and we teach children from school textbooks that we insist should be accurate, separating myth from reality. But the Epicurean analysis of knowledge as based in corrigible subjective experience and as dependent on human-invented categories and partially shared human evaluations implies that there is no such thing as a unique and full account of a historical event.

The realisation that there are multiple perspectives and points of view available has to accompany respect for evidence that stands up to scrutiny. Not only historical writing, but news reporting, which provides material for future histories, reflects what Epicurus called the need for 'choice and avoidance'. Writing history means writing a story, a narrative of connected happenings. This means deciding what will count as the event or period to be described, from whose point of view the story will be told, what will be included and what is peripheral, and how the decision and actions of the actors in the story are to be judged morally and practically, as wise, foolhardy, corrupt, courageous or brutal. For the most part, history textbooks still focus on battles, territory disputes, legislation and treaties. These choices imply that these events, and the people who played a role in them, are the most important things and people of the past, and that it is important to know the exact dates on which the events happened.

Meanwhile, a great deal is avoided in our curricula. To learn how people actually lived in previous centuries you have to pay to go to a museum or some kind of period entertainment complex, and you will quickly forget most of the information supplied. If you want to know what marriage and childrearing were like, what epidemic and occupational diseases people suffered from and how they were treated, why neighbours sued one another and what punishments were meted out for various crimes, or what it was like to be a front-line soldier or a textile worker, you won't learn this in school. You may never have the chance to learn it at a college or university either. Our decisions as voters and legislators would be far sounder if we knew more about the history of marriage, childrearing, the experience of warfare, sickness and labour practices, and could make meaningful comparisons. For the Epicurean, only the sharing of first-person perspectives and the recognition of their multiplicity can lead to sensible decisions in the public as well as the personal realms.

Today's Epicurean agrees with the ancient philosophers that an understanding of history and society is not arrived at by immediate perception. But he sees historical enquiry as aiming to remove bias and error and to widen its focus to construct a shared image of reality that reduces the temptation to introduce or maintain futile or hurtful practices. We should treat history as a rich and important source of information relevant for political decision-making, and recognise that it is narrated from a particular point of view about what is important. To reduce history to stories of kings and princes (and a few queens and princesses), prime ministers, presidents, chancellors and ambassadors, and to battles, defeats and victories, is to make a restrictive selection. To then evaluate political actions only in terms of the success or failure of prominent individuals in achieving their strategic goals, rather than in terms of their effect on human welfare, looks objective, when it is in fact a way of obscuring important truths. Although there are no alternative facts, there are alternative ways of using the facts there are to tell alternative stories.

10
WHAT CAN WE KNOW?

We must attend to present feelings and to sense-perceptions, whether those of mankind in general or those peculiar to the individual, and also attend to all the clear evidence available, as given by each of the standards of the truth.

Epicurus

I f the visible, tangible world is an appearance founded upon the imperceptible reality of atoms and void – or their modern equivalents – what do we understand by truth? How can there be truths that we can agree on that can guide us in our everyday affairs?

THE IMPORTANCE OF FIRST-PERSON EXPERIENCE

One of the oldest and most intriguing areas of philosophy is the theory of knowledge, or epistemology. Although epistemology has some esoteric aspects, the questions it deals with and their Epicurean answers can be explained simply and intuitively. These answers have implications for science, politics and religion that are discussed in Chapters 11–13 (pages 187–242). For now, I want to focus on our knowledge of everyday matters.

For the naive realist, as such people are termed in philosophy, the world is made up of tables and chairs, people and their pets, buildings, trees, rivers and mountains, cars and phones, and so on. We perceive the world via the five senses – seeing, touching, smelling, tasting and hearing – the naive realist maintains, and so get to know about the objects, events, situations and other people in the immediate vicinity. As long as you aren't blind, or near-sighted, or seriously astigmatic, and as long as you aren't hallucinating or suffering from an optical illusion, you see these things as they really are.

According to Lucretius, who is not a naive realist, we perceive ensembles of cohering atoms as everyday objects, people and features of the landscape, because these tiny particles blur. He offers the lavishly poetic illustration of looking at a flock of sheep on a distant hillside. 'Fleecy sheep crop the luxuriant pasture and inch forward wherever the tempting grass, pearled with fresh dew, summons them, while their lambs, replete with food, gambol and gently butt. Yet to us in the distance, the whole scene seems indistinct, appearing only as a motionless white blur on the green of the hill.' Qualities – the transparency of water, the yellow of a marigold – arise from the arrangement of the atoms composing them, and they change with our perspective and the light. So the sea, which does not change its underlying constitution, can appear many different shades of grey, blue, black, green or, when stirred up by the wind, white. The smell of incense and the taste of salt, the atomists claimed, arise from the action of odourless and tasteless particles whose shapes stimulate us in particular and individual ways.

What we call 'seeing' and 'tasting' is then really 'seeing *as*' and 'tasting *as*' and this opens up a troubling set of issues. I cannot take it for granted that objects look the same colour to you as they do to me, or that chillies or broccoli give us each the same taste experience. Who can claim to perceive the world 'as it really is'? If all perceiving is 'perceiving as', don't we all perceive a different world, and aren't there as many truths about it, many of them contradictory, as there are perceivers? If we could see the atoms themselves – the things that supposedly exist independently of our perceptions – we would still be seeing them differently. And seeing them would not help us to assess truth and falsity in the quality-laden world we actually live in. The modern specialist in particle physics will have no special professional insight into the qualities of different olive oils or grades of wool.

If you add all the factors of different upbringings and experiences to the differences in basic sensory equipment and the different levels of motivation people have when it comes to making fine discriminations, it seems that no one can claim to perceive the world as it really is by using their five senses. The problem of objectivity becomes even more serious when we consider the influence of our constitutions, experiences and interests on our perceptions. How can disagreements between individual people, political parties or nations ever be resolved if the contestants are perceiving different worlds from a variety of perspectives?

Some philosophers have argued that truth can only be found in areas of human knowledge that don't depend on the use of our senses, or on our personal memories and reading habits, and that don't engage our personal emotions. This leaves, at best, mathematics and logic. Unfortunately, mathematics and logic, if we were totally deprived of the use of our senses and could only make calculations and prove theorems in our heads, would be of no practical use to us. To apply mathematics and logic, to build bridges, to derive correct deductions from medical experiments, to keep track of money, and even to learn mathematics and logic in the first place, we need to see and to interact physically with a world of objects, people, events and situations and to be reasonably certain that we perceive things as they actually are.

And anyway, despite having no ability to perceive directly the fundamental reality of particles and forces, and despite the individuality of my sensory system, upbringing and past experience, I can reasonably claim to know a lot about the world outside my imagination. If I didn't know that there is a solid floor under my feet, I would be hesitant to take a step. I'm not hesitant, so I must know that. If I didn't know there was milk in the refrigerator, I'd be wondering whether to go shopping. But I know there is because I just looked, so I'm not even considering going shopping. My appreciation of what's the case in the world seems to be sufficiently good to enable me to nourish myself, travel on trains and buses, make repairs around the house and so on. Nor am I in constant (as opposed to occasional) disagreement with other people about tastes and colours, or about what just happened in the news and what it means. So obviously I do know many things, and a great deal of what I know is common knowledge shared with others.

Epicurus grasped this dilemma by both horns. Although perception is relative to observers and their positions, and although different observers often see things differently, first-hand perceptual experience of the world appearing to the senses is the touchstone of truth. It is, quite simply, the best we can do. If you yourself have experienced an event at close range, such as your neighbour's house burning down, you will and should believe it occurred. If another person reports to you that they have witnessed an event, such as your neighbour's house burning down, you may or may not believe them. It depends on whether you regard them as having been in a position to know, having no motive to deceive you and being well informed as to which house is your neighbour's. If you have any reason to doubt their qualifications as reporters or their honesty, you should not believe their testimony until you have made some further investigations. In general, claims that do not depend on first-hand experience, or on reliable testimony, should not be believed.

This position is known as empiricism and was adopted by many later philosophers. The empiricist rejects the claim that the human mind can have direct, intuitive insight into nature or, for that matter, into the supernatural.

Epicurus recognised that not all first-hand experiences reveal the truth. Square towers look round in the distance, and I might fail to see that what I thought was a horse in a field is really a cow. But he went on to point out that only the senses can correct the senses. I can correct my errors by getting closer to the object and noticing that, viewed from close up and from more angles, the tower is definitely square, and the animal is definitely a cow. I can also rely on your trustworthy testimony that the tower is really square. Ultimately, however, for my judgement to be true, the tower must actually look square to anyone with good eyesight who sees it from a better vantage point. The idea of 'optimal viewing distance' is vague and probably can't be defined precisely, but in ordinary contexts, we have a good sense of how close you have to be to a flower or a building to identify it for what it is.

RESOLVING DISAGREEMENT

If you and I have a disagreement about what is true, the usual way to determine who is right is by diagnosing and correcting for any distorting effects on our first-hand experience.

Suppose you think there is an odd smell in the room and I deny this. It seems there are various possibilities, for example:

1. You are imagining or hallucinating. There is no odd smell in the room.
2. I have a cold and cannot smell anything. There is an odd smell in the room.

We can often resolve disagreements by discovering that one or the other perceiver is not in a proper condition to be making sensory judgements. But what if:

3. I know you to have a more sensitive nose than 99 per cent of the human population? Is there an odd smell or not?
4. You are not imagining, hallucinating or a supersmeller, and I don't appear to have a cold or any other deficiency. Is there an odd smell or not?

The disagreement is now not so easily resolved. In option 3, your faculties for detecting odours are not defective. They are excellent. But they are not normal, so why should your abilities as a supersmeller determine what is the case? In option 4, try as we may, we just can't get to an agreement. Our dispute may be unresolvable, even after we've investigated our respective sensory equipment as far as possible.

Perhaps we can just agree to disagree on the grounds that it doesn't matter. You, the supersmeller, can leave the room to get away from the smell that only you can smell. Or I may oblige you by opening the window to clear the smell I can't smell myself. But our disagreement may escalate into conflict. You insist on opening the windows to clear the air, and I object because I am cold. Our different ways of perceiving the world threaten to unleash a quarrel. Now we are in competition over whose suffering is worse and more deserving of remediation:

your suffering from the smell only you can smell, or my being cold if you open the window to relieve it. Much household bickering involves perceptual judgements about appropriate clothing, well or poorly prepared food, unacceptable untidiness and other such seeming niceties. Tempers can run high when people see the world differently and come to believe that they are being victimised because of other people's supposed misperceptions of reality.

The moral here is that although no one can claim to perceive reality directly, disagreement about what is happening can have unfortunate consequences. Sometimes disagreements can be resolved and harmful practices avoided by identifying and discounting perception-distorting influences. But the two parties in a dispute may fail to reach agreement. For example, your teenager might think there are factors adversely affecting your judgement about what is appropriate to wear to school, namely that you are just out of it and have no recent experience of school. You think you are appealing to timeless standards of good taste. What looks slovenly or tacky to you looks like ideal schoolwear to them. Shouting, tears and headaches may follow. Not only is disagreement unpleasant, it actually matters who is right. Your good-taste standards may subject your child to needless humiliation; conversely, their obstinate preferences may in fact result in misjudgements about their abilities.

At this point, it is helpful to try to get a grip on causes and effects and on the fears that distort perception. Will your teenager really endanger him or herself by leaving the house dressed like that? Are they really setting a course of inappropriate clothing for life that ensures they will never get a job? Alternatively, could you relieve your mother's anxiety or calm down your father by wearing something else that would not really affect your status in school?

To be sure, answering these questions involves, once again, perceptual judgements about dangerous versus innocuous situations, reasonable and unreasonable anxiety, justifiable and unjustifiable anger, and so on. But as long as both parties not only value the pleasure of harmony over conflict, but can agree that the aim of resolving the disagreement and adopting a course of action is to prevent inconvenience, distress and harm to others, there is hope.

Now consider a serious political disagreement. Much more is now involved than personal comfort and discomfort, embarrassment and anxiety. Other people's welfare now comes into the picture.

Political disagreements are based on perceptual judgements and usually involve fear. Do you see the world as stocked with freeloaders and parasites, with inferior people and infidels? Conversely, do you see the capitalist class of bosses, bankers and entrepreneurs as ruthless exploiters who keep their subordinates poor and ignorant? Do you think women are threatening to take over in some way that will render men oppressed and miserable at home, at work and everywhere else? If so, you will have strong opinions about politics that bring you into community with those who see the world as you do and into conflict with others who do not.

Suppose *I* see the government as coddling the poor and diminishing their incentive to work by means of handouts such as food vouchers. Suppose *you* see the government as stepping in to save lives where the market has been unable to provide acceptable jobs. If I am right, this practice of giving out food vouchers is socially harmful and ought to be stopped. If you are right, this practice is socially helpful and ought to be continued.

Here are some possibilities:

I have not acquired my views from spending time among people who receive food vouchers and seeing with my own eyes the negative effects the food vouchers have had on them. Nor are my views derived from talking to reliable witnesses who work in poor neighbourhoods, or from reading the statistical reports of those who have studied the relationship between poverty and social programmes at first-hand. Rather, it simply appears blindingly obvious to me that handouts create dependency, and the people I talk to and the articles I read confirm me in this opinion.

You have not derived your views as to the beneficial effects of food vouchers from first-hand experience or from reliable witnesses or specialists who have studied poverty and social programmes at first-hand. Your views are just based on your general soft-heartedness and some crime shows you watched on TV where hungry and demoralised people were unable to find work and look after their children and were being victimised by landlords and gangsters.

Although you and I may never meet and may never experience a disagreement, since we each only talk to people who think as we do, it matters who is right. There are two reasons for trying to find out who is right, or more right. First, because social conflict based on different fears and perceptions is itself deeply unpleasant; and second, because, if we have equal power to influence policy by running for office, or supporting candidates for office, or just voting, we have the power to change the balance of pleasure and suffering, for the food-voucher recipients and for the taxpayers, by dismantling the food-voucher programme or by supporting and strengthening it. As in the earlier case, we need to adopt a critical attitude towards our respective fears and look for hard evidence that they are justified or unjustified.

When a dispute about what to do based on different perceptions becomes impossible to settle, it's time to look for hard evidence about causes and effects. One policy or the other may already have been tried. Were the circumstances similar, and if they were, what actually happened? Or an experiment may have to be made for the first time and the outcome noted. Do people actually become more motivated and find gainful employment when we take away their food vouchers? Do their children get enough nourishment to learn in school and to make their own contributions down the road? Do the taxpayers really reap the benefits and enjoy better lives thanks to their tax burden being reduced, or do they barely notice the savings and find themselves even more burdened by crime and police costs?

The answers to many such questions are available to anyone who makes a search for them. We know, for example, that poverty has diminished in the UK over the last twenty years, thanks chiefly to the provision of old age and unemployment benefits and the housing allowance. We also know that after decreasing in the US in the 1990s, thanks to similar social programmes, poverty has increased dramatically since the rollback of welfare in the current century. The number of people living in US ghettos and slums has nearly doubled since 2000.

To take another example, consider the current US debates about gun control and the fears and perceptions that are creating serious social conflict. Referring to abstract principles of freedom, revering decisions taken centuries ago in entirely different circumstances, and bringing in fanciful speculations about the potential need to mount armed resistance against the government or the Internal Revenue Service cannot put policy in touch with current reality. To enable us to decide what legislation to pass, we need hard evidence about murder and suicide rates in countries with strict gun control and countries without it. We also need, for comparison, hard evidence about how many persons have saved themselves from likely murder or grievous harm thanks to the possession of a firearm. This information needs to be presented repeatedly in legible and memorable format.

But more will be needed to resolve this long-running argument. The aim of the Epicurean is to mitigate fear, pain and anxiety. To plan the best course of action, she demands statistics and graphics, but not only statistics and graphics. She wants to hear from people who are afraid to go to sleep without a gun under their pillow, from people who are grieving a young child killed in a gun accident, and from teenagers whose schools are now staffed with armed guards.

The most important political discussions of our time concerning poverty and violence share a common structure with seemingly trivial disputes over allegedly stuffy rooms and allegedly inappropriate school clothes. Perceptual judgements are at work in each case and it is not surprising that people can experience the world in such different ways. Because our individual perceptions *feel* so true to us as individuals and our personal fears *feel* so well founded – and because, as Epicurus thought, experience is the touchstone of truth – these social disputes are difficult to resolve. And while not much can go wrong from mistaking a cow for a horse or a round tower for a square one, perceptual errors in family life and politics can have the most painful and destructive consequences. Although there are alternative perceptions, there are no alternative facts. Although *neither* of the two parties to a factual dispute may be entirely right in what they maintain, *at most* one of the two parties in a factual dispute can be entirely right.

Is Empiricism True?

Empiricism is an attractive doctrine, but, when interpreted too simplistically, it faces several objections:

First: The truth of empiricism can't be perceived by the senses. Epicurus says we should accept it, but why should we trust his testimony? So isn't empiricism self-refuting if it claims that the senses are the basis of all our knowledge and that we should accept only testimony that ultimately traces back to first-person experience?

Second: Scientific theories refer to objects like 'quarks' and 'gravity waves' that no one has ever seen, or felt, or otherwise experienced. In fact, much of science seems to be worked out by pure reason. This includes atomism itself. Should the empiricist reject science?

To the first point, it has to be agreed that there is no way to prove the truth of empiricism by means of the senses. And it would be absurd to try to produce a rationalistic argument for why empiricism is the right way to test our beliefs. Does this mean empiricism is a matter of faith – that we have to accept that Epicurus revealed its truth to us? This, too, seems absurd.

The best response to this dilemma is to say that empiricism is not a claim that is itself true or false, but rather, as the philosopher Bas Van Fraassen maintains, a stance I can *choose* to adopt. One reason to adopt it is pragmatic. The policy of trusting my first-person experience has been hugely successful in keeping me alive and reasonably well contented. I trust my eyes and ears as to when I am in dangerous traffic, or threatened by an animal, and I trust my bodily sensations as to when I need food, water and shelter. My senses inform me as to which foods I will likely enjoy, what perfumes I should choose or avoid, how to furnish a room attractively, and my subjective feelings inform me as to whether a film is worth watching to the end. I will take other people's testimony on these matters more or less seriously, depending on how reliable I believe them to be as witnesses.

Another reason to adopt the empiricist stance is that I welcome many innovations, such as the development of drugs and medical techniques, that depended on detailed first-person observation, experiment and reliable testimony. The pace of innovations accelerated when empiricism was rediscovered and redeveloped in the period known as the Scientific Revolution. This period coincided with the appreciation of Epicurean philosophy. So there is nothing self-refuting about adopting empiricism as a stance that is advantageous for human life.

To be sure, empiricism has not been an unmixed blessing. The power over nature that the adoption of the empirical stance has produced has brought many ills upon us that we would not have suffered if physics and chemistry had remained in a pre-17th-century condition. There are some things it might have been better not to know, such as how to manufacture atomic weapons. The empirical stance will doubtless lead us to knowledge of how to create test-tube animals, new viruses and new methods of surveillance and thought-transference, and once you know how to do something it is very difficult not to do it. What kind of knowledge we ought to seek and what we do with the knowledge we have are important ethical questions.

The second problem with empiricism concerns the unobservable nature of many scientific entities, including the Epicurean atom itself. As the previous chapter showed, the inference to the existence of atoms depended on an analogy (dust motes in the sunbeam) and on observations like attrition and abrasion.

Although scientific instruments like microscopes and telescopes can compensate for some limitations on our perceptual abilities, useful knowledge is often acquired through leaps of the imagination and long chains of reasoning. Charles Darwin's theory of evolution by natural selection depended on analogies and extrapolations, and no one until recently ever claimed to have observed the emergence of a new species. We most certainly do not experience an attraction between every mass in the universe and every other mass, but Newton proposed his theory of universal gravitation as the best explanation for the motion of the planets around the sun, and he was justified in doing so. We usually need mathematical and statistical analysis to reveal non-obvious cause and effect relations that we can't perceive even with microscopes and telescopes.

The Epicurean regards theories about unobservable entities as provisional. At the same time, as I will show in the next chapter, the scientific consensus deserves respect. Science arises out of a tradition that was committed to removing sources of error in our subjectivity and those arising from inadequate conditions of perception.

PART IV

THE SELF IN A COMPLEX WORLD

11

SCIENCE AND SCEPTICISM

*There would be no advantage in providing security against
our fellow men, so long as we were alarmed by occurrences
over our heads or beneath the earth or in general by what
happens in the boundless universe.*

Epicurus

*In the study of nature, we must not conform to empty
assumptions and arbitrary laws but follow the promptings
of the facts; for our life has no need now of unreason
and false opinion.*

Epicurus

Political security – what Epicurus calls 'security against our fellow men' – consists in freedom from fear of military attack and losing one's own life, or losing friends and relatives, in battle, as well as freedom from rape, robbery, intimidation by police and overly harsh punishment by the legal system. It consists in the absence of anxiety over the availability of food, shelter and medical care; the confidence that these will not be withheld from us by greedy others. In the absence of these forms of political security, no one can have a very good life; they are the precondition for most forms of enjoyment.

But political security is not the only form of security we need, as Epicurus points out. Much that happens 'over our heads', including the weather, and much of what happens 'beneath the earth', including the extraction of oil, plutonium and diamonds, diminishes human security. So does much that happens within our own bodies.

As far as the ancient Epicureans were concerned, they could never really be sure why the things over our heads, such as eclipses, lightning and tornadoes, and the things 'beneath the earth', such as earthquakes, happened. Nor could they predict their occurrence or control them. Yet, believing that they were explicable in physical terms, that they were not caused by supernatural powers, conquered fear. The movements of the sun, moon and stars, they claimed, did not prove the existence of powerful divinities needing to be pleased and revered to keep things going, and natural disasters did not indicate that these gods could punish mortals for mysterious reasons and needed to be appeased with sacrifices. Except where the movements of the sun, moon and stars were concerned – in fact a real problem for the atom-based theory of nature – the ancient Epicureans had a bottom up as opposed to a top down perspective on what happens in the world.

Scientific explanation of things above, below and on the surface of the earth is important for us today, because, unlike the ancients, we can predict and control much of what happens in the world, where prediction and control are based on our knowledge of the 'atomic' reality underlying the appearances. As a result, we have far more opportunities for choice and avoidance, both on a personal and on a political level, than they did. Yet the conceptual problem the ancient Epicureans ran up against – the fact that natural occurrences depend on causes too small and too complex to be directly observed by human eyes – faces us as well.

Today, even though the pace of scientific and technological advancement is unprecedented, many people have become suspicious of the scientific claims we encounter on a daily basis in the media. There are several reasons for this. First, scientific reporting in the newspaper is often sensationalistic and inaccurate. Too many supposed breakthroughs never amount to anything, and dietary and drink advice seems to reverse course every week or so. Hallowed formulas, such as the injunction to drink eight glasses of water a day, turn out to be mythical inventions.

Second, we are increasingly aware of how much of past science was distorted by assumptions of racial and ethnic inferiority and other forms of bias, and new contributions to the age-old genre of intrinsic inferiority literature continue to appear. Third, scientific knowledge has become increasingly monetised in production, dissemination and uptake. The financial interests of the pharmaceutical and medical device industries, agribusiness, tobacco and the energy-producing sector are now interwoven with scientific research in a way they were not in the past. Industry-sponsored studies of efficacy and safety have been put in doubt by more independent investigators. As a result, we have good reasons to be sceptical about some alleged discoveries, as well as good reasons to be sceptical about scepticism about some actual discoveries.

Today's Epicurean strikes a balance. She recognises that figuring out exactly what is going on at the micro-level is remarkably difficult. Scientific 'proof' always falls short of logical certainty – the sort of certainty that allows us to infer *for sure* that if all cats are mammals, and Caroline is a cat, Caroline is a mammal. (In case you want to argue that if Caroline is a toy cat, she isn't a mammal, I am on your side, but you will have to get into the technical literature on semantics and logical inference to defend that claim.) Scientific opinion undergoes many shifts, and nowhere is this more evident than in the many inconclusive discussions of lifestyle and disease that I will discuss in a moment. Sometimes it turns out that the experts were wrong. But ignoring scientific consensus because it doesn't meet the elusive standard of logical proof is irrational. Before moving on to the contemporary issues of diet, climate change and evolution, here is a brief account of the Epicurean approach to scientific explanation.

Scientific Explanation

According to the Epicureans, tiny, invisible particles in combination and interaction with one another are responsible for the most familiar phenomena in nature. Here is how they believed things worked:

Scents and flavours: Particles of particular shapes are
   soothing to the nose or mouth and therefore pleasant;
   or rough, or jagged and therefore unpleasant.
Dreams: The same 'films' emitted from objects that enable
   us to see them get mixed up and drift into the heads of
   sleepers.
Reproduction: Particles drawn from every part of the male
   and female parents mingle during sex and serve as
   scaffolding for building the body of the offspring by the
   addition of further particles.
Diseases: Toxic seeds or germs are particles that disrupt
   the structure and motion of the particles composing the
   body, causing it to malfunction.

While these explanations do not entirely hold up today, some being closer to the mark than others, the assumption that what happens at the level of everyday experience depends on microscopic goings-on is the basis of modern science.

It is sometimes pointed out that little particles don't explain everything. Little particles don't explain why square pegs don't fit into round holes, or, for that matter, why triangles have three sides, why 2 + 2 is four, or why sacrificing your queen is usually, though not always, a blunder in chess. Little particles don't explain why your sister's daughter is your niece. Nor do they explain the origins of the First World War. But if you look aside from mathematics and from social phenomena to chemistry, biology and medicine, little particles explain most of what happens in the world.

The formation of a snowflake, the development of autism or schizophrenia, the events leading up to heart attacks and climate change, are molecular. Consciousness must depend somehow on the behaviour of micro-particles, and if ESP turns out to be possible, there must be an explanation for it in terms of the entities and forces postulated by physics. These entities will not be solid objects, as envisioned by the ancient atomists, and the forces will not be those of impact and resistance, but they will be all natural. We would understand how phenomena like these arise, and, in some cases, how to intervene in their production if we could only grasp what is happening at the micro-level.

The Epicureans realised that because the atoms they posited were too small to be seen, they could not know for certain the true explanations for complex phenomena. Many possible but different explanations could be proposed, and no single one could ever be conclusively verified as the unique and true explanation. And there's the rub. If everything depends on what the atoms of nature (whatever these ultimate units really are) are doing, and if they lie outside of our direct perception, how can we get to know about them? Isn't science a matter of conjecture and of what we think in the end is most plausible? And if so, is science really so different from religion?

The question is complicated, and the answer to it is important, because choice and avoidance depend on what explanations we take to be correct. For the ancient Epicurean, although it was important to show how the phenomena might be explained, getting to the unique, true explanation just did not matter because human hands could not manipulate nature either at the astronomical level or at the atomic level. It was enough for them to be persuaded that everything that happened had a natural as opposed to a supernatural cause.

For us moderns, however, getting to the right explanation does matter. We are in a completely different position. We can't control the sun, moon and stars to suit human interests, even if we could see some advantage to, say, brightening or dimming the moon, or turning the temperature of the sun up or down a notch. But we have achieved enormous control over the micro-world, having worked out, over the centuries, what kinds of particles actually exist, how they can be combined and decoupled, and what they can do in combination.

The particle-based theory of chemistry underwrites all modern manufacturing processes from the ancient arts of cheese-making and dyeing, to drug development, plastics and bomb-making. All this was entirely unanticipated by the ancients. Their ethics did not address the problems raised by the power of modern physics, chemistry and physiology when it comes to changing the course of nature. Their epistemology did not envision the introduction of scientific instruments and methods and the complications involved in ensuring that we have really arrived at the right explanation. For if you have 'explained' something, but explained it the wrong way, and you try to control it, you will probably fail in the end, and you may create a lot of damage.

CAN WE TRUST THE SCIENTISTS?

Between the 1980s and the turn of the century, heart specialists were virtually unanimous in recommending that people give up butter and switch to margarine. Butter is an age-old milk product that has been consumed by humans for millennia. Margarine is a synthetic invention made from hardened vegetable oil, defatted milk powder and artificial yellow colouring that originally was meant to address the problem of wartime shortages of animal fat. Butter, it seemed, contained fatty cholesterol particles that stuck to the insides of our arteries until, like drainpipes, they became blocked, and an explosive heart attack ensued. Margarine, it was thought, must just break down into components that slide right through.

This theory was highly plausible. It was easily visualised by anyone who has ever dealt with a clogged kitchen sink and widely accepted, and some statistics appeared to vindicate it. But heart attacks among people who substituted margarine for butter actually increased, and the hydrogenated trans fats in margarine were discovered to be more harmful than butter. Since then, these fats have since been banned in many localities, and margarine-makers have changed their formulas.

Further investigation revealed that the experiments with rabbits and the observational studies on which the pro-margarine recommendations were based did not justify the conclusions drawn, and the physiology of atherosclerosis was revealed as more complicated than the drainpipe model indicated. The researcher most credited for recommending margarine, Ancel Keys, was discovered not only to have used hydrogenated margarine as a proxy for butter in his experiments, somewhat negating their point, but to have ignored data that did not support his hypothesis. The sugar industry had seized on his published claims and provided financial incentives to several Harvard University researchers to point the finger of blame away from sugar and refined carbohydrates and towards saturated fat in the genesis of heart disease.

The former consensus that eating saturated fats including butter causes the deposition of cholesterol in the arteries is giving way to the suspicion that atherosclerosis is an effect of inflammation, with the body laying down fatty particles to try to protect the artery walls. But the jury is still out on the seemingly basic, easily answered question: what kind of fat, and how much of it, should I eat to remain healthy as long as possible? Butter, as it turns out, contains trans fats.

The best way to answer the question from a scientific point of view would be to match up two groups who were identical to one another in all relevant ways and force one group to eat prescribed quantities of possibly dangerous Fat A and another to eat prescribed quantities of possibly dangerous Fat B. We would then check their disease conditions and whether they were still alive on a regular basis over a long interval of twenty or thirty years. But ethically we can't experiment on people in this way, by forcing them to adhere to a particular diet for such a long time. Further, from a practical perspective, we don't know what the relevant ways are for matching the two groups, and people don't always know what is in their food. Researchers therefore try to identify groups that match on characteristics such as age range, sex and average weight. They look at what people report eating, under the doctor's advice, or of their own free will, and they check the outcomes. Physiological models are then constructed to explain the outcome in, just as Epicurus thought, the most plausible fashion. We do not, however, ever get certainty out of this procedure. We can only hope that as more relevant variables are identified, more models prove testable, and as more people trial provisional recommendations, science can move towards a new consensus.

If you look up the professional medical literature, you will note that studies purporting to show some health effect (such as the harms or benefits of soy protein for the brain) are often contradictory. Alcohol, according to researchers, seems to have both neuroprotective and neurotoxic effects. Changing the type or quantity of fat you eat might reduce your chances of having a heart attack, but increase your chances of cancer or dementia. Many conclusions have to be rejected because they are based on poorly designed studies, or studies that enrolled too few subjects, or that permitted consequences to be drawn only for a small group of people – for example, middle-aged Finnish men. Researchers, like dentists and hairdressers, like to criticise the last effort as methodologically a botched job.

The prudential question, 'What fat, and how much of it, should I eat to remain healthy and happy as long as possible?' is still impossible in the 21st century to answer with certainty as long as we lack full knowledge of the micromechanics of the human metabolism. The current consensus nevertheless favours the Mediterranean regime of brightly coloured fruits and vegetables, fish, wine, beans, olive oil, and small amounts of meat and bread that sustained people for thousands of years. Epicurus might have considered this array somewhat luxurious, especially with the wine and fish, but it is both pleasant and prudent. Ancel Keys himself lived to be 100. According to the obituary in the *New York Times*, he followed a Mediterranean diet with plenty of olive oil, presumably lacking in margarine.

In the Seventies and Eighties, ignoring the dietary advice of doctors, including cardiac specialists, on what new product to spread on your toast and sticking to the former favourite, butter, would have been the best policy. This is true in the case of many other medical scandals, where dangerous drugs, or futile, unnecessary or disabling surgery were recommended by specialists. You may be surprised at the level of scientific controversy that actually exists over the risks and benefits of such popular interventions as statin therapy and mammograms. Reducing cholesterol levels, for example, has a protective effect against cardiovascular disease in a select group of people but unfortunately does not lead to a longer life for most people.

Should the Epicurean of today be habitually sceptical about the advice of experts and stick to old habits as long as the recommendations to change have not won unanimous agreement from the scientific community and acceptance of the results by industry?

Take the case of climate change – and what is happening 'over our heads'. The thirty-one-year-old Intergovernmental Panel on Climate Change critically reviews published research on the causes, progress and social impacts of climate change. The consensus is that the earth is getting warmer because of the emission of invisible particles of carbon dioxide into the atmosphere from industry and transportation. This process can be slowed or reversed by controlling the emission of these particles. The mechanism by which the additional carbon dioxide produces global warming is well understood. The predicted effects of climate change include the spread of tropical diseases and infestations to formerly cooler climates, disruption of agriculture, flooding in some regions, water shortages in others, and increased displacement of animals and people, migration and armed conflict. A small minority of climate scientists denies that man-made climate change is occurring. None of them denies that temperatures have risen since the Industrial Revolution, but they maintain that other causes are at work and that controlling the emission of carbon dioxide would have no effect. They point out that for certain periods in our history the earth was in fact much warmer than it is now. (Wheat once grew in Greenland.) They maintain that warmer temperatures and more atmospheric CO_2 will prove a boon to agriculture, that other predicted effects are speculative scare-mongering, and that nature will adapt as it has in the past.

So maybe the climate-change denying minority, like the few defenders of butter over margarine we can imagine were around in the 1970s, is right?

In neither case, fat or climate, can we just wait and see what the consensus is after another twenty-five years of research. The personal issues of choice and avoidance face us now, as we decide whether to reuse and recycle or not to bother, whether to give up the car and whether it is prudent to buy shoreline property. The political issues of choice and avoidance face legislators and voters determining energy policy and pollution control regulations.

An important feature of science is that it improves its methods for designing experiments and series of observations, and for analysing data, as well as improving its breadth of data. We demand multiple studies, reviewed for their sampling biases and the logic behind their inferences. No researcher today would be persuaded by Ancel Keys's original reports on margarine versus butter.

Where climate change is concerned, high-quality evidence is available. The claim that the warming trend is innocent or beneficial and that nature is constantly changing anyway is naive. Warming trends were not as devastating in the relatively under-populated 12th century when it was easier for populations to move. Today, the problems posed by the displacement of people in the poorer regions of the earth and their competition over scarce resources are massive. Climate change is a moral issue because it involves real harm. We in wealthy nations benefit most from the processes leading to carbon emissions, and the wealthiest of us are the most able to shield ourselves from the costs of global warming. The burden is already falling on the poor and powerless.

While roughly half of the US population now follows the scientific consensus in accepting manmade global warming as fact and sees the need for changes to legislation and household habits, only about 20 per cent of recently surveyed people at all educational levels, from high-school graduates to those with postgraduate degrees, follows the scientific consensus in believing that humans evolved without any divine oversight of or input into the process. The other 80 per cent, including some scientists, believe that God created human beings in their present form or guided the process of evolution. Do we risk doing our students a disservice when we do not present the theory of intelligent design side by side with the theory of evolution by natural selection as its active competitor? Or would it be harmful to do so?

Darwinism, when updated by modern biology, proposes that the frequencies of genes (tiny, subvisible entities) change because some living organisms possessing them fail to thrive and reproduce, in the environments in which they find themselves. Changes in the frequencies of genes produces changes in the appearances, inner workings and behaviour of plants and animals. The Epicureans, as discussed earlier, anticipated the idea of selection, and, with the addition of the discovery of these units of heredity and the concept of variation, Darwinism was eventually accepted as the right account – the right general theory, if you like – of the origin of the existing species and the extinction of many in the past, rather than as 'mere speculation'. The empiricist accepts this result, even though no one has ever observed, from a first-person standpoint, the evolution of humans from apes, or of any species from any other species.

Darwinian evolution is an unsettled theory in the following sense: not all researchers agree that all evolution depends only on chance variations arising from random mutations in genes with fixed programs, followed by selection. In fact, Darwin himself did not suppose that all variation was due to chance.

Epigenetics is a current area of research that demands that we abandon genetic determinism, as well as simplistic ideas about the existence of single genes for complex traits like intelligence, or the appearance of diseases like dementia. Like 'athletic ability', these manifestations depend on the environmental triggers that turn genes off and on, as well as the balance of positive and negative contributions of many genes. The decisions we make, as well as the environments we are involuntarily subjected to, can affect our own genes and those of our descendants. Epigenetic effects are nevertheless ultimately to be explained in terms of the same physics and chemistry that underlie other regions of human physiology; they are broadly consistent with the Darwinian account.

The upshot is that we should keep an open mind about the range of causes of speciation and evolution in plants and animals that builds on and corrects what has been established up to now. The challenges posed to Darwinism by proponents of intelligent design, such as the problem of gaps in the fossil record, or the alleged fine-tuning of the fundamental constants of physics, should be discussed and the responses to them evaluated. There is no intellectual or moral risk, however, in ignoring intelligent design in biology classes, and there is both intellectual and moral risk in teaching it as a live option. Intellectual integrity demands that it be presented, respectfully, as a formerly compelling view that has been superseded by a more empirically adequate option. For moral reasons we need to combat the view that the fate of all plants, animals and humans resides with a loving and intelligent deity who will surely order everything for the best.

LIVING WITH UNCERTAINTY

To conclude, our everyday experience of the world, and of what happens to the people and things in it, shows us some causes and their effects, but most causality is hidden from us. As Epicurus and Lucretius pointed out, what happens in the microworld concerns our vital interests, yet we cannot directly observe the hidden micromechanisms at work in the human body and in the rest of nature. Natural systems are complicated, and scientific disagreement can be expected whenever invisible processes are involved. Where the experts disagree, there are likely many factors at work needing to be disentangled in order to separate causes from correlations.

If there is a strong and determinate cause-and-effect relationship between any two events that can be directly perceived with ordinary vision, we are likely to be well aware of it and to know whether to exploit it or prevent it. It is common knowledge that most liquids to be found in the garage and under the sink can be drunk only with the direst consequences. But there is much that we can't see, taste or feel that can harm and help in ways that are not common knowledge. As noted, this applies to pollutants in the air and drinking water, to chemicals in household products, cosmetics and food packaging, to radiation, pesticides and herbicides, and nanoparticles. It also applies to the life-preserving (and the toxic) particles in fruits and vegetables and the possibly deleterious molecules in meat existing alongside nutritious particles, and the damaging properties of sugar molecules, which also produce very pleasant taste sensations and energy.

We need to be aware that invisibility and complexity, and so the absence of common knowledge based on first-person experience and reliable testimony, offer opportunities for manipulation and deceit. Manufacturers would like you to believe certain things about the causal powers of their products, whether they actually have these powers or not, and they would like you not to know about certain causal powers they know their products actually possess. Do cigarettes have the power to give you a nice sensation once you are used to them? It is common knowledge that they do. Do they have the power to make you more attractive to potential mates? Usually not, but the manufacturers would like you to think so. Do they have the power to give you numerous diseases and disabilities? Yes, and the manufacturers would rather you think this doesn't apply to you personally.

Contemporary controversies over fossil fuels, over genetically modified organisms, over the use of psychoactive drugs for depression and over vitamin supplements all depend on the invisibility of the little particles of matter that make up everything around us and the very indirect methods we have to employ to figure out what they are doing. And in every case, enormous financial profits and losses are at stake, depending on what we as consumers choose and avoid. When you have to evaluate how harmful or beneficial some practice or substance is, look for the most up-to-date information you can. Look at how both sides respond to criticism of their claims and whether they can address criticism satisfactorily. Ask yourself who stands to benefit financially from people believing and acting upon one claim or another, and how powerful those beneficiaries already are.

12

SOCIAL JUSTICE FOR AN EPICUREAN WORLD

Kings began to build cities and to choose sites for citadels to be strongholds and places of refuge for themselves; and they distributed gifts of flocks and fields to individuals according to their beauty, strength, and intellect ... Later wealth was invented and gold discovered ... [T]he situation sank to the lowest dregs of anarchy, with all seeking sovereignty and supremacy for themselves.

Lucretius

A free life cannot acquire great wealth, because the task is not easy without slavery to the mob or those in power ... And if [one] does somehow achieve great wealth, one could easily share this out in order to obtain the good will of one's neighbours.

Epicurus

The Epicurean story of humanity tells us that our modern governments emerged by degrees from the kleptocratic regimes that seized property, displaced the natives of the conquered regions, demanded tithes and handed out lands, titles, incomes and influence to their personal favourites. Competition between rulers devastated the lands and properties and took the lives of men, women and children who had no part in these quarrels. Some rulers were genuinely beneficent and fair, but it has been only through popular and philosophical pressure that governments have evolved into servants of the people even to the extent that they have.

Remembering where government came from is important in understanding where it is now and where it could go. Power, money and favouritism, the Lucretian trio of forces that can be turned against humanity, continue to operate where they see opportunities, benefiting selfish, amoral individuals and groups. Today these forces work against the best interests of the populace, blocking or discouraging investment in public goods, such as mass transit, universal healthcare, education and access to culture and to unspoiled nature.

Epicurean materialism is, to my mind, a sound basis for humane and enlightened political action. This may seem surprising. Some historians argue that the French Revolution, not only in its idealistic early stages, but during the Terror, when fury against the aristocracy and the clergy led to appalling bloodshed, was inspired by 18th-century materialist philosophy. Some of the worst atrocities in 20th-century history were perpetrated by Joseph Stalin, the author of a book called *Dialectical and Historical Materialism*. Rather than looking irrelevant or antiquated, Epicureanism can appear irresponsible, unrealistic and dangerous.

What can be said in its defence? To answer this question, I would like now to look more closely at Epicureanism's positive and progressive influence in earlier eras when political leaders and legislators were well read in philosophy and the classics.

Around the beginning of the 19th century, the English jurist and philosopher Jeremy Bentham, declaring that 'mankind is ruled by two masters, pleasure and pain', succeeded, to a considerable extent, in purging corruption from law and administration and in reforming, to some extent, the barbaric English prison system. Bentham argued that tradition and religion should not determine law and public policy. The only relevant question to ask when a policy is being debated, he declared, is: will implementing this policy contribute to the greatest good, in terms of freedom from pain and provision of enjoyment, for the greatest number? John Stuart Mill, another admirer of Epicurus, wrote and spoke in Parliament influentially on free speech, the emancipation of women and the reform of poverty laws.

In the United States, a number of the 18th-century Founding Fathers were Epicureans who believed that the true function of government was to foster 'life, liberty and the pursuit of happiness', as opposed to the extension and defence of empire. In

1819, Thomas Jefferson, an enthusiastic reader of Lucretius, wrote to a correspondent, 'I too am an Epicurean. I consider the genuine (not the imputed) doctrines of Epicurus as containing everything rational in moral philosophy which Greece and Rome have left us.' Jefferson accused the traditional rivals of Epicureanism, the Stoics, and especially Cicero, of misrepresentation, hypocrisy and 'grimace'.

The major impact of Epicurean political philosophy was, however, through its development by three figures, each of whom was inspired to rethink the specific problems of his own society via the Lucretian history of humanity. The three philosophers I have in mind were: Thomas Hobbes, writing in the mid-17th century, who favoured a centralised government; Jean-Jacques Rousseau, writing in the mid-18th century, who favoured community-based democracy; and Karl Marx in the mid-19th century, who favoured worker ownership of all corporations. Their ideas are well worth revisiting for their potential application to the problems of our era.

THREE EPICUREAN PHILOSOPHERS ON WAR, INEQUALITY AND WORK

Hobbes was an Epicurean materialist who declared that 'All is Body'. In his own history of humanity, which he intended more as an illustrative fiction than as an anthropologically correct account, he ignored Lucretius's account of happy, sociable pastoralists in a golden age before civilisation and instead portrayed a radical jump from solitary foraging to a 'war of all against all'.

Lucretius's history explains that people grew tired of chaos and bloodshed and instituted laws and enforcers of the law to control it. Hobbes believed that this process had not gone far enough because government was not sufficiently centralised and effective. He had just lived through the English Civil War of the 1640s, and he believed that, in addition to ordinary criminality, thieving and physical assault, religious conflict and recurrent national chaos and bloodshed would be inevitable under the current system of government. To prevent this, he argued, everyone, especially fractious aristocrats seeking power for themselves and religious prophets who tried to stir the people up to revolution, ought to agree to submit to a single central authority. The only real responsibility of this 'Leviathan' would be to manage a peacekeeping bureaucracy; the expensive expansion of national territory was not, as so many princes and other crowned heads assumed, the purpose of government. With protection from interpersonal violence assured, manufacture, trade and travel would be fostered, making human life more luxurious and enjoyable. The tendency of modern nations towards the centralisation of power and the submission of individual nations to multinational authorities such as the UN and the European Court of Justice, and to multinational legislation, such as the Geneva Conventions, the Nuclear Non-Proliferation Treaty and the Paris Agreement on climate change, are Hobbesian in inspiration, and are to be welcomed.

In Jean-Jacques Rousseau's very different account, Hobbesian centralisation posed too much of a danger of autocracy and repression. Drawing heavily on Lucretius's history in his *Discourse on the Origin of Inequality* and in his *Social Contract*, Rousseau argued that political society should try to recover the archaic small-group equality portrayed in Lucretius's account of the golden age before the invention of agriculture and the formation of armies. The development of commerce and bureaucracy, Rousseau thought, had led to misery and oppression for the exploited and overtaxed peasantry and to decadence in the parasitic upper classes. Political decisions should be made with the common good as their aim by developing participatory democracies on a small, county-level scale. Luxury and enjoyment were not to be aimed at, but instead probity and virtue. Rousseau's critique and his utopianism have been echoed by eminent anthropologists like Marshall Sahlins, who contrasts the mentality of hunter-gatherers, 'the original affluent society', well satisfied with what they have, with the classical economists' view of the human being as a creature of almost unlimited wants and limited means to achieve them. 'To exist in a market economy,' Sahlins said, 'is to live a double tragedy, beginning in inadequacy and ending in desperation.'

The 19th-century philosophers Karl Marx and Friedrich Engels were engaged by the Lucretian idea that technological change led to fundamental social reorganisation. Marx had written a doctoral thesis on Epicurus, and Engels was a keen student of the history of science and materialist philosophy. Engels believed that Epicureanism's contributions to enlightenment were its commitment to 'the original goodness and equal intellectual endowment of men, the omnipotence of experience, habit and education, and influence of environment on man, the great significance of industry, [and] the justification of enjoyment'. Where Lucretius had focused on the control of fire and the invention of metalworking as driving social change, the particular innovation Marx and Engels focused on was 19th-century industrialisation. They appreciated Lucretius's point that, with the invention of money, the wealthy had come to exert all the political power in a society. Their solution was to apply Rousseau's democratic principles to industry. The profits of their labour should be returned directly to the people who were actually making the goods that created profit. Marx and Engels did not envision the rise of an oppressive, Stalinist, directive regime;

rather the nationalistic, warmongering 'State' was supposed to 'wither away'. Their ideals resembled modern profit-sharing plans, but without the modern skimming off the top by directors and investors.

As Marx made painfully evident, mass production requires most of the world's workers to perform work that is boring, repetitive and stressful, with the profits of their work going principally to the employer or his investors. The same is true of much modern office work. Enjoyment is deferred to evenings and weekends. By evening, however, most workers are exhausted, too tired to shop for flowers on the way home, too tired to cook a tasty supper, certainly too tired to indulge a taste for science or philosophy, and inclined to stun themselves with alcohol or drugs. Worker ownership of firms, Marx maintained, would distribute the wealth of a society according to the real capabilities and needs of individuals. Eventually, technological progress would transfer labour from human beings to machines, freeing up their time for a variety of personally meaningful activities. Marx imagined that instead of being based on monotonous, alienated factory and office work, the society of the future would be recreational and allow for individual whims and preferences. The utopia he described in one of his early manuscripts, in which I am able to 'do one thing today and another tomorrow, to hunt in the morning, fish in the afternoon, breed cattle in the evening, criticise after dinner, just as I have a mind', sounds like a version of the Epicurean Garden, though with more emphasis on quarry and livestock than our contemporary ethics favour.

No one denies that the capitalist system works better than a planned, communistic economy when it comes to stimulating innovation and making a variety of new and improved goods available for purchase. Just look at all the brands and styles of shampoo, toothpaste, eyeshadow and costume jewellery that you can choose or avoid. However, where, as Rousseau pointed out, human beings in the state of nature enjoyed their work – their hunting, gathering and handicrafts – most modern people do not. Both feudalism, in which a peasant class works for and is controlled by its overlords, and capitalism, in which nearly everyone is an employee, destroy personal autonomy, make our labour 'alienated', and prevent people from developing their innate intellectual, social and aesthetic capabilities. Those of us who do enjoy our work, most of the time, and who are able to enjoy a range of aesthetic and intellectual experiences, are extremely lucky. But we are a minority.

EPICUREAN POLITICAL PRINCIPLES

Although the Epicurean Garden does not provide a sustainable model for any economy, political will could move us in that direction. Reducing the length of the workday from the eight-hour shift punctuated by lunch and coffee breaks to two five-hour shifts, say from 8 a.m. to 1 p.m. and 2 p.m. to 7 p.m., staffed by different people, would not be popular with industry, which prefers to maximise output, minimise personnel and maximise their individual working hours. But it would boost the employment rolls, reduce economic inequality between men and women, solve the childcare problem and enable people to take up hobbies, cultivate specialisms, join groups, exercise, visit and entertain others, cook, play, gamble, read and engage in the range of human activities that civilisation is meant to offer us. Night-shift work between 7 p.m. and 8 a.m. could be abolished as constituting a cruelty towards members of a diurnal species whose children require night-time companionship. Less would be produced, less would be consumed and less would be thrown away. Living within such a system might nevertheless exemplify what Epicurus means by 'prosperity' – the state of prospering.

Few managers or governing boards are likely to strike out in this direction. But the examples just given of political reforms introduced, attempted or at least up for discussion show that if you have a taste and a tolerance for political action, you can reflect and act on Epicurean principles while remaining engaged in politics and commerce.

The politically minded Epicurean sees no benefit in economic growth or productivity as such. The only good policies, in her view, are those that can relieve hunger, illness, stress, fear, anxiety and inconvenience. For every proposal coming before the public and their representatives in a democracy – tax reform, gun control, health and safety regulations, transportation and housing policy – we should ask ourselves: is this proposal helpful? Will it relieve the most basic ills – lack of access to good food, clean water and air, a good education? Or is it likely to lead to more illness and loss of life? Is it aimed at enriching the already well off?

As noted earlier, the Epicurean maintains a generally sceptical stance towards rights and traditions. She recognises no natural rights, only rights that we decide should be enshrined in law and defended. Our decisions should depend on how the proposed right will have an impact on well-being, and this can change over time. For example, the Second Amendment of the US Constitution, as it is currently interpreted and enforced, represents a social decision. The decision is that the murder of helpless people and the massacre of entire groups of children by disgruntled individuals is an acceptable price to pay for the benefit of making it easy to purchase and own firearms. To the Epicurean, this decision is wrong for our time and place, especially when weapons of mass destruction are readily available to angry and desperate people. Empirically, the number of home-owners' lives saved by having a handy weapon in the house, assuming this is the most presentable justification for gun ownership, bears no comparison to the number of lives lost. According to a well-conducted study, for each instance of successful self-defence or justifiable homicide using a gun, there were twenty-two cases of assault or criminal homicide, unintentional homicide, suicide and attempted suicide using a gun.

But don't we need rights and traditions in addition to, or even instead of, calculations of pain and pleasure? Where rights are concerned, public executions might have brought a thrill of enjoyment to the crowd in previous centuries at the expense of just one person's premature death, but the state is often said to have no right to engage in murder. Many of us believe that torture cannot be morally justified, even if it reveals valuable information, which it rarely does, and that solitary confinement in prisons is and would be unacceptable, even if it had a deterrent effect.

In all these contexts, calculations of pains versus pleasures for the majority seem repugnant, and what Adam Smith and Immanuel Kant thought of as the sacredness of the individual seems to be the more fruitful and necessary concept. We even believe it would be wrong to take one cent from 100,000 people's bank accounts through internet fraud, to collect $1,000 to buy circus tickets for 100 poor children, even if no pain is produced by the former action and much pleasure by the latter. The right to a fair trial is one we might feel could not be sacrificed for any other good.

The Epicurean will respond that the right to a fair trial as well as other alleged rights are worthy conventions because they prevent large numbers of people from being harmed as they otherwise would be. But the right not to have money taken from your bank accounts, even for a good cause, and the right not to be tortured by the police when suspected of a crime don't refer to some mysterious property of personal inviolability. For the Epicurean political theorist, what we refer to as rights are firm decisions, based on estimates of the long-term consequences of permitting even petty theft on a mass scale or instituting torture as a permitted means of getting desirable information. We don't try to calculate costs versus benefits on an individual basis in handing out parking tickets, or try to decide what kinds of mostly unnoticed extractions from other people's bank accounts could produce joy; we just keep the rules as socially beneficial ones, unless it's decided to change or scrap them.

Can traditions justify political practices even when they harm people? The Epicurean thinks decidedly not; the fact that a law or practice has existed for a long time is not an argument for its moral goodness or even its moral acceptability. Restricting marriage to one male and one female is traditional, but many persons are harmed by the tradition, and the supposed benefits are also imaginary. It is hard to see how my marriage can be helped by preventing homosexuals from marrying. Female genital mutilation is an example of a traditional practice performed on girls too young to refuse it; the circumcision of male infants is another. The former has painful lifelong effects on girls and women. The latter causes pain to boys and may have other deleterious consequences later in life. The benefits achieved are not medical, as was believed earlier, but disciplinary, symbolic or decorative. While fitting in with others, and performing the surgery on the next generation might confer some kind of satisfaction, if the decision to be snipped and sewn were left up to the mature individual, these motivations would likely vanish relatively soon. Most districts restrict the symbolic or decorative

216

practices of tattooing and piercing to informed adults over eighteen and find willing takers, but the surgeries in question would not prove so popular.

To summarise, the engaged Epicurean will endorse many prohibitions that cite the fiction of human rights, as long as these rules are aimed at preventing and do prevent grave harm to individuals. She will insist that traditions should be reviewed whenever questions about them arise to verify that, overall, they are leading to good results without imposing pains and burdens.

JUSTICE FOR WOMEN: NATURE, HISTORY AND CONVENTION

Women have been much written about in Western literary culture in terms of fear, scorn, obsession, praise and affection without, until recently, having had a chance reciprocally to write about men in an evaluative manner. Alas, the philosophical writing of past centuries does not display much esteem for women's insight, judgement and fortitude, and Western cultures are not distinguished by their respect for their women's personal preferences with regard to education, occupation or choice of marriage partner. When Plato recommended equal education and physical training for girls and boys, it was widely believed he was joking. Aristotle held that virtue in a woman is entirely different from virtue in a man. For women, virtuous behaviour consisted in being quiet and obedient, while virtue in a man involved being courageous, truthful and generous. Housework as the most fitting female occupation, and chastity as the greatest female virtue, remained standard in the theory of women down to the 20th century, even in the very few philosophers who favoured equal education for women.

Epicurus claimed that there could be no relations of justice between humans and other animals. In effect, humans could only be cruel or kind to them, because the other animals were not part of our legislative communities. They were not capable of rational discourse leading to sensible agreements on limiting harm. Legislation, up until recent times, made the same assumption about women. The assumption was that there was no need to agree about laws and regulations *with* women because they were not part of the legislative community; all that was necessary was for men to agree on laws and regulations *concerning* women. These laws were both cruel and kind. They prohibited access to education beyond an elementary level, property ownership, voting, freedom of movement and choice of a marriage partner, occupation or profession. They also kindly provided for the financial support of dependent wives.

The restrictions and physical aggression to which women have been subjected in civilisation and the verbal derogation they have endured in philosophy and fiction have only been systematically studied by historians and social scientists since the end of the Second World War, though women's expression of their grievances goes back to the early days of print culture. Why is the status and treatment of women such a problem, one might wonder? Were women always 'second-class citizens' – or, more accurately, not citizens at all, but only subjects of their governments? These questions can be fruitfully explored by keeping in mind the Epicurean principles that convention is not to be confused with nature or necessity, that technological progress gave rise to new forms of oppression, and that relations between men and women should be both friendly and just.

Despite measurable differences in the various components of perception and cognition, it has been repeatedly shown that there are no significant differences between the genders in problem solving, creativity, general intelligence and task persistence. Yet even today, men generally believe that they are intrinsically more intelligent and more competent than almost all of the women they know. This is an error that is easily explained. The same superficial reliance on experience that infers intrinsic racial inferiority from observing and comparing different neighbour-hoods – ghettos versus commercial centres – infers sexual inferiority from observing and comparing men's and women's sizes and typical occupations. The antidote to error is a deeper empiricism that explains the appearances in terms of real, as opposed to imaginary, causal influences.

Women are somewhat smaller than men, not because they are underdeveloped or more childlike, but for a good reason: they need more calories in pregnancy and lactation and could not feed and maintain larger bodies. Though the average female brain is smaller than the average male brain, women's cerebral cortex is thicker and more convoluted than men's, features associated with cognitive competence. Yet women in the modern world populate the low-cognitive-demand service fields of cleaning, nursing, and clerical and retail work; even the virtual assistants of the internet age – Siri, Julie, Erica and the rest – are female. Men populate the executive and pundit ranks and collectively determine what is going to happen in commerce, law and politics.

Anthropologists nowadays agree that the transition from life before agriculture and metalworking to life within civilisation, as recounted in the Epicurean prehistory of humanity, explains many features of women's subordination. Especially in urban settings, where space and resources are at a premium, women's fertility is sometimes desired and at other times a burden and an embarrassment. The new efficiency in food production presented acute problems of overpopulation, as did the possibility of inheriting wealth, and the reproduction rates of a community could be more easily controlled by keeping women indoors and secluded than by trying to restrict the movements of men. Women's beauty and charm, and competition among men for the companionship and sexual fidelity of particular women, can lead to quarrels and bloodshed. Keeping women away from men outside the family circle or wrapping them in bulky clothes and head coverings to try to make them less attractive was another attempt to deal with the problems they were seen as causing. Setting the tone for many future Christian writers, the most famous of the Fathers of the Early Church, Saint Augustine, declared, 'What differences does it make whether it is a wife or a mother, when a man has to guard against Eve in every woman.'

Their greater upper-body strength made men better candidates as a group for soldiering, navigation and the control of draft animals; and their lesser role in childbearing and childcare made them better candidates for administration, scholarship and politics. The old division of labour in hunter-gatherers was succeeded by the new role-allocations of civilisation. The discovery that animals could be domesticated, fenced in and used for work as well as for food was followed by the discovery that human beings, too, could be fenced in and used as slaves, and that women could be so used by refusing them an education and keeping them indoors.

Philosophers were confident they could answer a question that it would never occur to an Epicurean to ask, namely, What are the purposes of men and women for which they were created? Aristotle pondered the difference between women and slaves, who seemed so much alike. Both groups were at the mercy of their masters; both took care of the maintenance tasks of the household; and neither group took part in the honourable and lucrative professions. 'Does a slave possess any other excellence, besides his merits as a tool and a servant?' Aristotle asked. 'Nearly the same question,' he observed, 'is raised about the woman and the child.'

Men's role in the universe, according to the consensus, was to contribute to and defend knowledge, wealth and culture, and women's role in the universe was to bear children and to provide nourishment, comfort and sexual gratification to adult men. This was seen as making the best use of everyone's abilities. So women have been regarded by the major philosophical traditions as useful for generating men, whose physical and mental exertions are held to provide the real value to society, and for doing the maintenance work for men to develop and express their abilities and talents as military leaders, artists, rulers, scientists and writers.

Why were these arrangements unjust in Epicurean terms, and why are they still unjust to the extent that they persist? To most of our ancestors, they appeared to be based on mutual benefit, achieved through the division of social roles rather than by force. But this appearance was deceptive in a number of ways. First, because female intelligence and inventiveness are in no way inferior to that of males, force, in the form of unjust laws, was required to maintain the division of labour by denying women education and access to the professions. Second, the supposed benefits of the division of labour are losing much of their lustre. Despite the many achievements of civilisation following from the division of social roles, the world has been brought and is being brought to the edge of catastrophe through male energy and inventiveness, untempered by the female diplomatic and care-taking skills. These skills are sorely needed in contemporary geo-politics as well as in local government and in business and education.

In an Epicurean political community, people are not seen in terms of their roles, functions and purposes, but as accidental products of nature. The principal role of the legislator is not to enforce social roles for the benefit of the privileged, as it was and remains in the most corrupt times and places. It is rather – as the great political theorists discussed at the beginning of this chapter believed – to protect the weak, and those disadvantaged by their circumstances, from the ambition and resourcefulness of the strong. This protection makes the free development of their capabilities, through education and experience, possible and reduces the gap between the weak and the strong.

Women need certain forms of protection because their smaller size makes them vulnerable to physical force, and because the greater claims on their attention and effort produced by childbearing make them vulnerable to exclusion and exploitation. But the purpose of protection is to enable them to move around freely in the world and to act freely. The forms of protection that are needed should not be confused with protection that has the opposite effect of reducing freedom and blocking opportunities. By recognising this we can reduce the gap between men and women in opportunities to participate in all aspects of human life that have value. 'Wealth', as Epicurus said, not only in the form of access to and control over money, but also in the form of political and cultural authority, needs to be shared. The gender that, collectively, possesses far too much ought to share with the gender that, collectively, possesses far too little. This is not only for the sake of the well-being of individual women, but for the good of the entire polity.

We should keep in mind that law-making is a historical process and that justice is not timeless, except in the sense that humans will always care about it. Our conception of what is just ought to change as we learn more about the actual effects of our laws and regulations on everyone affected by them. As Epicurus says, 'In general outline, justice is the same for everyone ... But

... if someone passes a law and it does not turn out to be in accord with what is useful in mutual associations, this no longer possesses the nature of justice.' With all the wealth and technology existing in the modern world, we can do far better than we do now at creating laws, institutions and practices that satisfy the Epicurean conception of justice as an agreement that prevents one person – or one entire group of people – from being harmed by another.

13

Religion From an Epicurean Perspective

*First believe that God is a living being immortal and blessed,
according to the notion of a god indicated by the common
sense of mankind ... For verily, there are gods, and the
knowledge of them is manifest; but they are not such as
the multitude believe ...*

Epicurus

*You may perhaps imagine that you are starting on the
principles of an irreligious philosophy [Epicurus's] and
setting out on a path of wickedness. But in fact, more often
it is that very superstition that has perpetrated wicked
and irreligious deeds.*

Lucretius

Epicurus's statements on the existence of God – or the gods – and religious behaviour are deeply puzzling. First, he tells us that we should believe what the majority of mankind believes: namely, that there exists an immortal and blessed divinity. Then he comments that 'the multitude' have an entirely false idea of God. Yet he reportedly advised his followers to join in on popular religious festivals, and to sacrifice to the gods 'piously and well'. He also advised his followers not to create any public disturbances by voicing their opinions on the topic of religion.

Greek polytheism assigned attributes and responsibilities to its major deities, including Zeus (supreme ruler), Aphrodite (love), Mars (war), Poseidon (the sea) and Athena (wisdom). The gods were understood as emotional and liable to anger and revenge, as having their favourites, as intervening in the lives of mortals to punish them or to confer benefits, and as sometimes acting capriciously. Outbreaks of human passion, plagues and the sudden eruption of wars might be referred to their whims.

By way of alternative theology, Epicurus posited the existence of a society of happy immortals living in their own world in the intercosmic spaces. These gods were free of the characteristics

Greek religion ascribed to its divinities. They were not competitive and jealous; they did not engage in intrigues; above all, they did not use human beings as their pawns in their rivalries or favour them or punish them. They most certainly did not start wars such as the Trojan War. In fact, the Epicurean gods paid no attention whatsoever to our world.

How does this strange theory of intercosmic immortals fit with Epicurus's doctrine that the senses are the basis of all knowledge? Obviously, he never saw these beings in their natural habitat. And how could the gods be immortal? They must be atomic entities, and everything atomic is perishable.

Perhaps Epicurus really did believe that although Greek religion was purely fictional, another kind of god existed. Or perhaps he intended that anyone who took his basic doctrines seriously would realise that his theory of the gods was nonsense. Because blasphemy was a serious crime in Greece, punishable by death (as it was in many later Christian cultures), he may have been advising his followers to engage in outward performances to the extent needed to stay safe from persecution by the authorities. Another possibility is that he simply wanted to present to people's imagination, for contemplation, the ideal of a blessed life untroubled by any form of anxiety, including the fear of death.

Lucretius, by contrast, comes across as a fierce and unambiguous critic of religious institutions and the belief in superhuman divinities. Either, we must suppose, he had access to lost texts of Epicurus in which the latter was more explicit about his philosophy of religion, or he saw reason to depart significantly from the views of his predecessor.

BELIEF IN THE IMAGINARY

As Epicurus implies, most of humanity holds beliefs concerning the existence of at least one, but often a number of supernatural beings who influence history and our personal lives and with whom we will have further interactions after death. They are believed to respond to some prayers and to appreciate rituals performed in their honour. Religion motivates action, not only worshipful and charitable action, but also persecutory and violent action. Even if fewer things that happen on earth are ascribed directly to supernatural intentions and powers than was the case in earlier centuries, participating in religious institutions by going to church, celebrating religious holidays and praying is widely seen as a duty and as making a positive contribution to human life. And we still have good reason to fear religious conflict and religious fanaticism and martyrdom as making a negative contribution.

People who have received a thorough grounding in the natural and social sciences are statistically far more likely to describe themselves as atheists than are non-scientists. Yet there are physicists, biologists and other scientists with respectable credentials who believe in the creation of the world in six days or somewhat longer, the immortality of the soul, and in Heaven and Hell. And many people who don't actually believe in any of those things prefer to describe themselves as agnostics rather than atheists, implying that they are unsure whether a supernatural person exists or not. (Unless, that is, they take agnosticism to be the position that the existence or nonexistence of such a person does not matter.) They may participate in religious practices and institutions or declare a belief in some form of higher power not to be identified with the divinity of any known world religion.

This level of uncertainty may seem surprising, but it is not incomprehensible, given the complexity of reasons for being involved with religion, which go well beyond a simple inability to explain everything in ordinary causal terms. And it is often pointed out that virtually all of what we believe about scientific matters has second-hand status. We trust that what is reported in scientific journals, and what makes its way into the 'quality' press and into school and university textbooks, accurately represents the observations and calculations of observers with no motive to deceive us. We also trust historians when they tell us about the politics of Ancient Rome or the battles of the Second World War, though their information is collected from a variety of sources that, it is hoped, trace back to first-hand observation. We trust anthropologists and archaeologists who interpret objects, rituals and myths belonging to cultures long extinct or inaccessible for us.

The habit of trust carries over into the religious sphere. Nevertheless, there are good reasons to disbelieve what we are taught in this connection. As the 18th-century philosopher David Hume asked, in connection with the New Testament reports of miracles, Which is more likely? That some purported witnesses two thousand years ago misreported what they had seen with their own eyes, or that the laws of nature were momentarily suspended? There have been no inexplicable astronomical, meteorological or physical events of the sort reported in holy books in modern times. The Epicurean always accords less credence to second-hand sources than to first-hand experience. He also accords less credence to earlier second-hand sources, whose reports were generated before the appearance of an explicitly critical culture that demanded verification, than to later second-hand sources.

These observations raise the following questions: Why is religion a cultural universal, even if every culture has its individual unbelievers? Why does belief in God persist even in cultures in which people employ sophisticated modern technologies and have no problem believing that physics and chemistry explain the weather and that germs cause disease? Granted that religion can foster ethical behaviour, would a world of atheists be any less ethically motivated than the existing world? And granted that religions can foster cruelty and violence, would a world of atheists be any less cruel and violent?

Some atheists find the very idea of a caring yet irritable super-natural person with superhuman powers, including the power to raise the dead, absurd. They cannot understand how rational people can believe in the existence of a God or the gods, or in incorporeal and immortal souls. A more enlightened – while still Epicurean position – is that although the conventional ideas of God or the gods are indeed mistaken, it is not difficult to under-stand why rational and in other respects well-informed people adhere to them. Before going on to consider what a world with-out religion might be like, let me take you through the four sources of belief in God or 'the gods' identified by the Epicureans. These are wonder, personal experience, fear and gratitude, and tradition and authority.

Wonder

How could the universe in its vastness, and this world, with its intricately organised and interdependent plants and animals, have come to be? What keeps the universe in existence and the sun, moon and stars in their regular courses? The cause of all this, we may feel, must lie outside of physical nature. It deserves our reverence and our gratitude.

Personal Experience

In meditation, prayer and reverie, and when facing crucial decisions, we often experience a divine 'presence', or feel that we are being guided and supported by a wise and caring invisible power. Saints and theologians have left written accounts of their sudden conversions, and in the late 19th century, the psychologist William James set out to study the universal features of religious experience. He was able to draw on numerous first-person accounts by ordinary people of the sense of being visited by a supernatural being, protected in moments of life-threatening danger, guided in making major life decisions, and having prayers heard and answered. Mystical experiences of unity, harmony and transcendence of the everyday are aroused not only by drugs, alcohol, music, dance and poetry, but also by religious prayers, chants and incantations.

Fear and Gratitude

Earthquakes, tsunamis, droughts and plagues, and the harm that comes to individuals through accidents and illness, are punishing. When something awful happens, it is easy to ask oneself, 'What evil did we (or I) do to deserve this?' It can seem that a powerful being who wants to test the faith of believers or to punish the wicked must have unleashed the misfortune. Conversely, when we or a family member recover from an illness, or when our personal lives are suddenly transformed for the better, we feel intuitively that a powerful being has intervened to help us.

Tradition and Authority

All cultures with writing possess holy texts or sacred writings describing the characteristics of divine beings and their record of interventions into human life. An entire culture of architecture, painting and music develops around these texts and the stories they tell. Rituals and religious texts for weddings and funerals, and special costumes for the clergy, such as robes, staffs and headdresses, become familiar elements of daily life or present themselves to us in magazines, illustrated books and the great paintings in museums. Authority figures teach children and remind adults to obey rules and regulations using the threat of punishment and the hope of reward in this or another life.

PIETY WITHOUT SUPERSTITION

Suppose we take it as granted that the satisfaction of each of these motives for religious belief has considerable value in human life. Can they play a role without involving the subject in erroneous beliefs and reprehensible practices?

Where wonder is concerned, what Epicurus calls 'piety' – which can take the form of a feeling of gratitude for the world's existence and for my existence in it – is not irrational, even if there is no one to be grateful to. It is worthy of wonder that the universe, with its order, regularity and beauty, could just appear. It feels miraculous, in some moments, that life, with its complexities of metabolism, regulation and reproduction, consciousness and intelligence, could emerge from combinations of chemical elements like carbon, hydrogen and oxygen. The beauty of shells, feathers and foliage makes them seem, as the philosopher Kant commented, as if they had been made for our pleasure in looking at them. Yet Epicureanism insists that, as miraculous as it might seem, nature alone has brought all this about without any purpose or intention.

It is actually harder to think out how a mind unconnected with hands and without any pre-existing materials to work with could make the whole physical universe than to accept that everything comes from nature. That any of us exist, and that we exist in a world like this one, is a matter of chance, or at least coincidence. Nevertheless, had the fundamental forces of nature not been what they were, and had conditions on our planet been different, we would not be here to be in a state of wonder.

Where experience is concerned, the human mind seems to be predisposed to expect to be in communication with other human-like minds with good and evil intentions. We experience silent voices in our heads that seem to belong to an interlocutor who warns and advises, voices that are sometimes experienced as real. Wild animals, which our ancestors needed and feared, and even springs, groves of trees and strikingly shaped rocks can seem to harbour spiritual qualities. Hallucinogenic drugs can create perceptions of 'another reality' existing behind or alongside the everyday one.

Some writers maintain that Epicurus regarded dreams as a form of sense perception and that he often dreamed about the gods. Lucretius in turn claimed that religion developed because people hallucinated and dreamed of the gods. '[E]ven in remote antiquity, the minds of mortals were visited in waking life and still more in sleep by visions of divine figures of matchless beauty and stupendous stature.' They assigned the gods a habitation in the sky, and fearful of the might of the heavens, 'They took refuge in ascribing everything to the gods and in supposing that everything happened in obedience to their will.'

These experiences of mystery, beauty and power are intimate and valuable, but for the Epicurean, they don't imply the actual existence of another reality.

Fear and gratitude are also basic human emotions that are the foundation of our social life. We are constantly on the lookout for minds with intentions in active bodies that could be dangerous for us or helpful to us. I am acutely aware of it when a mosquito is trying to bite me, a territorial dog is threatening me, or another person is rushing to help me when I have dropped something or tripped. As a consequence, when we feel mysteriously helped or harmed, and do not see another living agent who is likely responsible, we suppose that an invisible agent, powerful enough to act at a distance without being seen, is the cause of our salvation or misfortune.

Escaping a serious traffic accident, or falling ill with a rare disease, can make it feel as if a helping hand has suddenly reached down from on high or that an offended superpower is inflicting punishment from somewhere beyond the ordinary world. Societies and individuals may carry a burden of guilt for what they see as their own offences against others, and guilt implies a sense of being watched and judged. Much Greek drama that still enthrals spectators deals with the experience of being under a curse.

We need to be aware of how deeply fear and gratitude are impressed into our psychology and to recognise our dependency on others, while refusing to infer from our experiences that they arise from a supernatural source. All our misfortunes and all our benefits flow from the nature of things. We are assuredly watched and judged by other people and by our own consciences, but not by morally concerned beings who exist outside the ordinary world.

Finally, tradition and authority. All cultures need to teach children ethical behaviour and to remind adults of their responsibilities to others. This is often accomplished in a religious context, because children want to know *why* they shouldn't lie, cheat, steal and abuse others and also *what will happen* if they do and are not observed by a punitive adult. It is efficient to tell them that all their actions are observed by an invisible being who has rules and who enforces them. Adults are subject to the same temptations, and churchgoers in Christian cultures seem to appreciate being told repeatedly of the joys of Heaven and the horrors of Hell that await them if they conform to morality or refuse to.

Religion is not only a vehicle for teaching ethics; it is also a framework for socialising and celebrating with other people, for reinforcing feelings of community, for communicating the seriousness of marriage and death, for unleashing artistic creativity in decorating houses of worship and costuming their personnel, and for giving a subject matter to painters and composers. So even people whose sense of wonder is satisfied by natural science, who do not believe that their transcendental experiences really arise from another world and who recognise ordinary human society as the source of their fear and gratitude may still value religion on account of tradition and authority.

Is there any point, though, to engaging in religious practices such as praying, singing hymns, reading holy texts, celebrating religious holidays or observing religious restrictions on diet and behaviour? Is there any point to or justification for these activities if you believe the books on which they are based to be human inventions and the divinities to which they refer to be fictitious?

This question can be answered from two perspectives: with regard to personal pains and pleasures, and with regard to morality. If you are bored or philosophically offended by sermons, and visit houses of worship only out of habit, the Epicurean advises you to do something more enjoyable. If you can enjoy religious activities and practices despite your unbelief because of the beauty of churches and temples, the pleasure of singing and the company of friends, if you find the dietary restrictions sensible, there can be no reason not to participate in them except moral reasons.

This is an important exception. Moral considerations may move you to join a church or to leave one.

CAN RELIGION BE IMMORAL?

Morality cannot be derived from religion, according to the Epicurean, insofar as the holy texts with their behavioural commands are human inventions with no special authority, and the prophets who claim to have been instructed directly by God were enjoying a special kind of experience that did not in fact have the cause they supposed. Accordingly, every religious practice has to be evaluated in terms of help and harm. Many religious practices are physically painful and, for the Epicurean, to be avoided, rather than chosen, unless there is a definite long-term benefit to enduring them. Sacrifices, mutilations and mortification fall into this category. Punishments mandated by holy texts, such as executing unbelievers and suspected sorcerers and stoning adulterers, are morally unacceptable to the Epicurean as such persons either do not pose a real threat or the nature of the threat is seriously misunderstood. Unlike malicious criminal behaviour involving predation on the unsuspecting public, adultery is in most cases the violation of an agreement between two people intended to prevent the torments of jealousy, not an offence against society.

In Book I of *On the Nature of Things* Lucretius launched a forceful attack on religion as fostering cruelty. In his history of humanity, he bemoaned the origins of religion in our ancestors. 'What sorrows did they then prepare for themselves, what wounds for us, what tears for generations to come!'

After praising Epicurus in the first book for liberating humanity, 'grovelling ignominiously in the dust, crushed beneath the grinding weight of superstition', Lucretius went on to paint a pitiful portrait of the sacrifice of Iphigenia, 'a sorrowful and sinless victim'. According to the Greek myth, the subject of a cycle of tragic plays by the 5th-century-BCE dramatist Euripides, Iphigenia's father, Agamemnon, the King of Mycenae, offended the goddess Artemis by killing a sacred deer. In order to bring about a favourable wind for the Mycenaean fleet to sail to fight the Trojan War, Artemis demanded the sacrifice of his daughter, and Agamemnon after much mental anguish gave in to persuasion. A young life was lost for the sake of a delusory belief in an offended goddess and her dictatorship over the winds. Lucretius argues that priests exploit fear of divine power and wrath to maintain political control over the people. 'Consider how numerous are the fantasies they can invent, capable of confounding your calculated plan of life and clouding all your fortunes with fear.' By threatening the population with eternal punishment for impiety and disobedience, they keep them ignorant and docile.

Are Lucretius's accusations justified? To be sure, religious beliefs and religious institutions have brought about much that is morally good. The churches have taken on the charitable work of caring for the poor, the elderly and the orphaned, when this has been neglected by the state, and many priests and ministers have helped individuals to find their way out of their personal difficulties and mental torments. Some religious texts have lent themselves to contemporary arguments for equality and tolerance. The anti-slavery movement in the 19th century in Great Britain and the US was driven by religiously inspired reformers like William Wilberforce and John Woolman, and the Reverend Martin Luther King and the southern churches of the US were instrumental in the civil rights movement of the second half of the 20th century. Dorothy Day, who founded the Catholic

Worker Movement, was a powerful voice for social justice in the 1930s. And Christian pacifists have been active in the modern anti-war movement.

At the same time, Lucretius's view that religion is a powerful and dangerous instrument of social control that exploits human credulity needs to be taken seriously. Drawing on his observations, we can see that there is a good deal of truth in his accusations.

First, clerics are supported economically by their communities, and historically they often used their offices to become rich as well as influential. The magnificent palaces of bishops in the early modern period rivalled the opulence of secular princes. The Christian churches acquired vast quantities of land by imposing certain laws governing marriages and inheritances, and enriched themselves by corrupt practices such as selling 'indulgences' or tickets out of Purgatory and into Heaven. Television preachers in our own time have amassed personal fortunes by soliciting donations from their devout audiences, and the prestige and protected status of priests allowed the sexual abuse of children to escape detection for decades.

Second, by preaching the sinfulness of mankind and threatening Hell, clerics have terrorised children and induced unnecessary guilt and conflict in individuals. Instilling the conviction that disobedience to one's political superiors, put in place by God as his representatives, has arguably kept populations humble and docile, unawakened to the reality of their situation, when they ought to have been rebellious.

Third, religion is a source of powerful ideas that can motivate hatred and violence towards 'the infidel', allegedly to please God and follow his commands. Crusades, jihads and terrorism arise from a mixture of political and religious motives. Although warfare would not be eliminated if holy texts and priests were to disappear from the face of the earth, one set of rationalisations for violence would disappear.

Fourth, the belief that God is in charge of human history can delude people into thinking that all political decisions made by their legislators – from exterminating the native population to altering the tax code in favour of the rich – must be good because they would not happen if they did not reflect God's will and his plans for the future.

Fifth, the belief that God gave the earth and all its plants, animals and other features to man, who was created in his image, has been taken as a licence to do to nature whatever satisfies human desires for property, fuel, raw materials, metals, diamonds and meat, regardless of the damage done to landscapes and living beings.

None of these features of existing religions – venality, intimidation, crusading, historical fatalism and speciesism, along with the antifeminism mentioned earlier – is, however, intrinsic to religious piety as understood by Epicurus.

CAN A RELIGIOUS PERSON BE AN EPICUREAN?

Although Christian writers in Europe from the early medieval period onwards professed alarm over the Epicureans' denial of a creator god and their views on the mortality of the soul and sexual pleasure, there were certain areas of overlap between early Christianity, as it existed before the creation of a vast bureaucratic power structure, and the Epicureanism of the Garden. Besides the obvious parallel between the pattern of leadership and friendship, including friendship between men and women in both systems, the historical Jesus was remarkably non-judgemental in everyday matters regarding pleasure. Epicurus's declaration that nature has provided us with all we really need is echoed in Jesus's advice to 'consider the lilies of the field'. His friendship with the 'fallen woman' Mary Magdalen might be compared with Epicurus's friendship with the 'courtesan' Leontion. Both moral philosophers rejected the prevailing norms of their culture, and neither one had any interest in ritualism, divination and priestcraft, or the accumulation of wealth. The Epicurean doesn't do things for the sake of money once she has reached a modestly satisfying level of personal pleasure in food, drink, apparel, furnishings and recreation, and neither does the good Christian. The values of equality and tolerance are not logically tied to a belief in the supernatural or to the authority of holy texts. At the same time, an important feature of religion is that it can defend and often, though not always, does defend moral values at odds with those of corrupted political regimes.

Most world religions enjoin their followers to shun at least some kinds of pleasures, even when it is not actually imprudent or harmful to others to indulge in them. In this regard, they are at cross purposes with Epicureanism. Nevertheless, at the heart of religion is a feeling that is probably universal: the feeling that our actions are observed and evaluated for their moral worth even when no other human beings are around to observe and evaluate them. 'God' is the name for the source of this universal feeling. Although Epicurus did not identify divinity with conscience, in saying that the gods exist because everyone believes them to exist, he can be understood as pointing to the fact that religious beliefs and feelings are part of the basic human psychological make-up.

To be able to look with an appropriately critical but not overly dismissive eye at religion, we need an alternative picture of reality, and this is what the ancient Epicureans tried to furnish with their account of how the universe and its living inhabitants came to be, the nature of the human mind, the nature of morality, and how to choose and avoid. The Epicurean distinguishes between the superstitious elements of religion in its culture-specific stories about the gods, their attributes and their doings, and the core truth that prompted the human imagination to tell these stories, the truth being that morality matters to us.

14

THE MEANINGFUL LIFE

*And so human beings never cease to labour vainly and
fruitlessly, consuming their lives in groundless cares, evidently
because they have not learned the proper limit to possession
… And it is this ignorance that has gradually carried life out
into the deep sea and has stirred up from the depths the
mighty boiling billows of war.*

Lucretius

*He who has learned the limits of life knows that it is easy to
provide that which removes the feeling of pain owing to want
and makes one's whole life perfect. So there is no need for
things which involve struggle.*

Epicurus

Epicurus taught in his Garden, purposely avoiding the markets and law courts of the city. Business and politics, he knew, were not conducive to philosophical tranquillity. In the Garden, greed and love of power and domination were absent, and knowledge-seeking, friendship between equals and moderate enjoyment gave daily life its shape.

How can an Epicurean life be lived in the very different environment of today, you might wonder? If we are not to live on other people's charity or at the expense of the state, we need to sell our physical and mental abilities to our employers or directly to the public as entrepreneurs. Even in the altruistic professions – medicine, education, some branches of law and administration – we have to engage in the rough and tumble and get along with strangers. If I even have a garden, I have to buy tools, fertilisers, pesticides, gardening gloves, and all this takes money. All of us have to make plenty of concessions to those in power and to go along with what the democratic majority decides to do.

And what if everyone tried to do as Epicurus did? Wasn't there something parasitic in leaving business, politics and defence of the city to others. Wasn't he foreshadowing the 'turn on, tune in, drop out' movement of the 1960s that urged its followers to ignore the workaday world and mainstream society and to enjoy blissful drug-induced states of intoxication focused exclusively on their private perceptions and thoughts? Rather than effecting lasting social change, that movement proved so fragile and irrelevant that it was soon reversed by the 'greed is good' ethos of the 1980s.

Further, a critical reader might insist that there is an important distinction between a *pleasant* life and a *meaningful* life that Epicurean philosophy ignores.

Pleasure in food, drink, warmth and companionship is available to any social animal, but we don't usually think of sparrows, dogs, horses or chimpanzees, social animals that enjoy their food, drink and the presence of their conspecifics, as having meaningful lives. The anti-Epicurean, Stoic-influenced Immanuel Kant claimed, 'We do not assess the absolute value of the existence of the world by reference to [human] well-being or enjoyment (whether bodily or intellectual) – in a word, happiness.'

Rather than setting out the conditions for a meaningful life, isn't Epicurus saying that we needn't be concerned with meaningfulness at all? Both he and Lucretius advise us to stop struggling and to find contentment in ourselves and in what we already have. But how can such passive enjoyment connect us to what Kant called 'absolute value'?

TWO CONCEPTIONS OF THE MEANINGFUL LIFE

What distinguishes humans from other animals is not the possession of an immortal soul, but the ability to commit oneself through belief and effort to abstract ideals, to transform ideas into reality and to pursue long-term goals in concert with others. Two main conceptions of the meaningful life that have been taught and defended in Western culture draw on this observation. The Epicurean of today sees the point of both, but she also regards both as liable to exaggeration and distortion.

In one conception, worldly achievement makes an individual's life meaningful. In the other, the one to which Kant himself subscribed, it is moral or spiritual effort, that, with luck, results in moral or spiritual achievements.

In the worldly view, the best sort of life involves *doing* something or *being* something that earns admiration and respect from other people. In this view, getting promoted to the top ranks of an organisation, earning a large pay packet and acquiring multiple dwellings, becoming a noted athlete, musician, actor or artist, or inventing a useful device like the electric light bulb, are all ways of assuring a meaningful life. The great artists, writers, conquerors, scientists and philosophers, such as Michelangelo, Shakespeare, Alexander the Great, Einstein, Socrates and a number of others, have had the most meaningful lives.

In this conception of meaningfulness as recognised worldly achievement, most people, especially women, fail to have meaningful lives, as they never distinguish themselves in any of these ways, though those who do are deservedly revered.

In the moral–spiritual view, wealth, power and worldly achievement do not make life meaningful. Rather, the meaningful life is one of service and sacrifice, whether it is noticed and praised or not. By sacrificing pleasure, and perhaps even health or life itself, and devoting oneself to the care of other people and the improvement of their conditions, one achieves the best sort of human life possible. In this view, anybody, male or female, regardless of family background and luck, can have a meaningful life. For while achievement, fame and fortune are not entirely under the control of the individual, service to others and martyrdom are available to anyone who chooses them. Firefighters, nurses and charity workers have more meaningful lives than bankers; and Mother Teresa and Albert Schweitzer are some of the best models we have.

In both of these familiar views, meaningfulness is understood as linked with our distinctively human characteristics: the meaningful life is seen as compatible with endurance and hardship, and even to require them. That is why both the 'achievement' and the 'service' ideals are so compelling: not only do they tell us what kinds of experiences and actions are meaningful, they also warn us to expect troubles and obstacles in pursuing these ideals.

The Epicurean agrees that it is the exercise of our specifically human capabilities that creates feelings of meaningfulness, and that achievement and service are both concepts that can help to orient us in life. Yet more, he will insist, is not necessarily better. In former centuries, some of the most admired persons were warmongers whose achievement was the massacre of thousands of people and the redrawing of national boundaries, and whose service was to the fatherland. This inference can be read off from the statuary of most major European cities celebrating the achievements of people who ruined towns and villages and ordered hundreds or thousands of young men to their deaths. In our century, some of the most admired persons are entrepreneurs who discovered how to profit from the monotonous labour of others and how to tempt consumers into buying unnecessary objects. The Epicurean looks with dismay on the selfish pursuit of glory and money. At the same time, she does not consider it to be obligatory for her to dedicate her life to others at the expense of her own health and enjoyment. Both excessive ambition and excessive self-sacrifice, she believes, distort human life. We should neither strive for pre-eminence nor be driven into or choose slavish self-abnegation.

To see how the Epicurean conceives in positive terms of the meaningful life, it is helpful to step back for a moment and think about the very idea of 'meaning' and 'meaninglessness'.

Meaningfulness for the Individual

The most immediate experience of meaning and meaninglessness most of us have is the connection with our native language and our disconnection with unknown languages. I recognise *my* native language, one in which words and sentences have meaning, as the one in which I express myself, guide others and am guided. It is easy to get around in places where my native language is spoken and in which I and others understand one another. A foreign language I don't understand is just noise or babble. It is discomfiting and frustrating to be surrounded by speakers you can't understand and to be unable to make your needs and wants known, when you are trying to obtain food, a room for the night or directions.

The meaningful poem, story or film has analogous features. It uses language and images that resonate with me, rather than discomfiting or frustrating me. I feel understood by it; it is as though the author could see into my own heart. I claim it as in some way belonging to me, as a favourite. With what are, to me, meaningless films, stories and poems, nothing much happens. I don't have the impression that whoever made them understands me or that they can give me insight or helpful direction.

By analogy, a meaningful life is one that I can identify with or can wish to make my own. It involves a sense of ownership, recognition and acceptance. The depiction of a meaningful life can guide or inspire me. As meaningful words and experiences provide what feels like an opening onto a wider reality, meaningful actions link my agency to that wider reality. So it is understandable that merely eating and drinking, even with enjoyment, and hanging around with friendly others, does not seem to be enough for meaningfulness.

The most satisfying activities in life are those that substitute knowledge for ignorance and that bring order and beauty into the world, repairing damage and overcoming disorder. A life can be good in Epicurean terms, even if it does not involve achievements validated and rewarded by mainstream society, or great sacrifices and struggles against worldly temptations. It is not necessary to conquer a country, or to rise to the top of an organisation, or to purvey soap or biscuits to the crowned heads of Great Britain. Whatever field you are in, you don't need the Pulitzer Prize, the Nobel Prize, the Purple Cross, the Keys to the City or to be on the cover of *Time* magazine to have a meaningful life.

What distinguishes humans from other animals is not the possession of an immortal soul, but the possession of these capabilities, grounded in the exceptional size and configuration of the human brain and its relationship to our hands. Lucretius calls attention to human inventiveness in making and using tools and to human artistry. This inventiveness does not require genius or even talent in the usual sense. Figuring out how to stabilise your roof rack can be a gratifying discovery in the course of an afternoon. The exercise of craftsmanship, whether it's putting together your lawnmower out of the box or organising your sock drawer, brings order and beauty into the world, satisfies the creator and may give pleasure to others even if it does not dazzle them or involve enormous sacrifice.

Services to others need not be undertaken on a heroic scale. You are not responsible for the whole world, and the people with whom you live need to do their fair share in the maintenance tasks of ordinary life so that you are not overburdened. Remember that justice arises from agreements, not traditions, and negotiate for fairness. Volunteer because your conscience drives you to it or because you get real pleasure from it, as most of us do, but if it makes you grit your teeth to go to PTA meetings or bake cakes for them, don't do it.

What makes life feel meaningful is doing what you are able to do to a certain standard that you set yourself, caring for those whom you like and love and being cared for by them. You can enjoy a gratifying sense of accomplishment that takes little or nothing away from other people. Music performance, for example, can be a highly competitive arena with jealousy, prizes, despondency, good and bad reviews, and requiring large financial investments in training, equipment and travel. Some have the appetite for this, but your personal involvement with music is no less intense and meaningful if you play with your second-tier community orchestra rather than with the Berlin Philharmonic. For little or no financial outlay, you can become fascinated with and immersed in challenging games such as bridge, chess and go, or, if that is not your thing, by taking dance or drawing classes, or learning another language.

Although Epicurus professed to see no value in learning things for their own sake, he wrote thirty-seven short books on topics as varied as kingship, language and astronomy. The Epicurean finds meaning in learning about the natural and social phenomena around him, following links to science, the humanities, the arts and politics, and deepening his understanding of poverty, disease, the climate, the rise and fall of stock markets, the history of the earth and the behaviour of animals.

If all this sounds exhausting, it is worth asking whether the pursuit of glory or money on the one hand, or enslavement to other people on the other, are taking up too much room in your life.

THE PROBLEM OF AFFLUENCE

The Epicurean distinguishes carefully between the personal enjoyment of food and drink on the one hand and gluttony on the other, between delights that are unlikely to bring on harsh pains or trouble for other people and those that are. Collectively, we should make the same distinction. Yet those of us in the affluent nations are collectively approaching the world as gluttons, rather than as thoughtful, pleasure-maximising, pain-minimising Epicureans. The glutton eats far more than is required to nourish himself enjoyably. Only some of what he eats nourishes his body; the rest is stored as fat or excreted.

The industrialised world looks less and less like Epicurus's Garden and more and more like the habitat of a glutton. Mainstream economists urge us on to growth, to increasing the rate of throughput that transforms raw materials – oil, coal, wood, metal, fodder, grains and water – into energy, consumer goods and foodstuffs, and that then transforms consumer goods into trash, much of it toxic or nearly indestructible. Rusting scrap metal and old machinery litters the outskirts of towns and cities and the countryside; an island of plastic bags covers 30 square kilometres of the ocean. Effluents, including heavy metals, the residues of pesticides and herbicides, mercury compounds, radio-active waste, PCBs, coal-tar derivatives and all the poisonous by-products of manufacture, mix with air and water. The more subterranean fuels and minerals are brought to the surface, the more the surface is erased. The land and the oceans are getting to be much too hot. These misfortunes were not planned. They simply came about as side effects of the development of new technologies and new economic and social systems.

Book I of Lucretius's *On the Nature of Things* opens with images of spring and the (figurative!) goddess Venus releasing her powerful shafts and injecting 'seductive love into the heart of every creature that lives in the seas and mountains and river torrents and bird-haunted thickets'. Book V ends with praise for the achievements of civilisation, 'gradually taught by experience and the inventiveness of the energetic mind'. These achievements included: 'navigation, agriculture, city walls, laws, arms, roads, clothing and all other practical inventions, as well as every one of life's rewards and refinements, poems, pictures and polished statues of exquisite workmanship ... People saw one thing after another become clear in their minds until each art reached the peak of perfection.'

Book VI, however, after a scientific discussion of thunder, lightning and other weather phenomena based on Epicurus's atomic accounts, moves to a discussion of poisonous substances and deadly vapours, including those emitted by burning charcoal in a closed room and by certain trees, and those encountered in mines. The chapter concludes with a grim description, with images of rot and collapse, borrowed from the ancient historian Thucydides, of the plague of Athens of 430 BCE.

The plague was probably a haemorrhagic fever similar to today's Ebola. Lucretius describes the ominous warning symptoms of the disease: 'the ears besieged with buzzings; the respiration rapid or ponderous; the neck bedewed with glistening beads of sweat, the saliva thin and scanty, salty and flecked with yellow'. The sickness progressed with 'ghastly ulcers and black discharge from the bowels; or else a flux of purulent blood'.

People mutilated themselves to try to stop the progress of the infection, but to no avail. Bodies piled up unburied in the streets, and sick people filled the public squares, 'their languid limbs half dead, caked with filth, covered with rags ...' The plague cut a huge swathe through the population and led to a breakdown of morals and public order as panic and opportunism took over.

The metaphor of the sick state was familiar in political writing, and Lucretius may have been implicitly referring in these passages to the cruelty of his own period, in which a recent and bloody civil war, slave revolts, executions and conspiracies furnished the background. He was perhaps also making the point that not only our lives, but all the achievements of civilisation can be destroyed in a matter of hours, days or weeks by tiny atomic entities.

We modern people face our own version of the sick state in the form of the ailing world. These problems look overwhelming and intractable from the individual perspective. Nevertheless, by forging cooperative relationships with others, by appealing to the nearly universal human desires for security, beauty and fairness, and by seeking to resolve political disagreements by being open to experience and experiment, human beings can emerge from a state of helplessness and paralysis. As a philosophy of 'choice and avoidance', presupposing human free will and the power to change laws and institutions when their harmful effects become evident, Epicureanism can embolden us to make principled and prudent decisions.

To that end, we need to look individually and collectively beyond the microrationality that saw each successive step as an improvement and evaluate the macrorationality of how our systems now work as a whole. We need to reduce the incentives to overspecialisation, overwork and too much consumption of energy and manufactured objects and textiles that abounds in almost every culture influenced by technology. We must choose and avoid from among the would-be political leaders, distinguishing between the truly prudent, who care about humanity's long-term future and who can take an objective perspective on nature and society, and the selfishly power hungry who ignore or reject empirical knowledge. We need to distinguish between those who are genuinely concerned with the common good and those whose so-called morality implies nothing more than the persecution of homosexuals and women seeking abortions.

Despite dismaying lurches in the opposite direction, we have made political progress since ancient times, much of it in the last few hundred years. The problem of military aggression, it is increasingly realised, must be treated as a problem of criminality that can only be addressed by the controlled use of force by a duly constituted police authority. The model of political and economic national interests that is held to justify aggressive interventions into other countries' affairs is increasingly regarded as obsolete. The notion of 'non-offensive defence' – maintaining the power to repel attacks that Epicurus recognised as necessary without creating tense situations that lead to war – is discussed in some elite military circles. Conventions such as the Geneva Convention, anti-proliferation treaties governing nuclear and chemical warfare, and multi-national accords reflect the Epicurean conviction that justice emerges from negotiation and agreement.

With not only human welfare, but the welfare of all life in mind, we have begun to adopt measures on a global scale directed at the preservation of oceans, forests, the atmosphere, soil, water and the climate, and the plants and animals threatened with extinction. We increasingly resist claims to the effect that prolific use of natural resources and the resulting pollution are indexed to the general welfare, or that conservation and regulation will promote general misery, recognising these claims as emanating from selfish interests. Consumers have insisted on formal standards precluding cruelty to and the exploitation of humans and animals, as this occurs in the industrial production of food, clothing, drugs and cosmetics.

New conventions have also been introduced that have facilitated the flow of women, homosexuals and ethnic minorities into the professions. We have made progress in understanding and remedying the harms done to and suffered by disfavoured social groups, including the indigent, prostitutes, addicts, the disabled, the elderly and prisoners, whom we were formerly inclined to regard as undeserving and of no account. Householders have come to novel agreements – social contracts on a small scale – about how to divide childcare and the work of cooking, cleaning and repairing and maintaining possessions, so that women's intellectual, artistic and political abilities and interests can find expression.

THE PHILOSOPHICAL PERSPECTIVE

Many people feel the need for a more cosmological, if not a religious, perspective if life is going to be experienced as meaningful. The desire to feel cosmologically important is however hard to satisfy because we are not. We inhabit one small planet circling one star in one galaxy of about 250 billion stars set in the midst of about two trillion galaxies. Assuming with the Epicureans that there is life elsewhere in the universe, indeed conscious, aware, so-called intelligent life, there is nothing special about our situation in the cosmos, which is in any case of limited duration. We earthlings are fascinating to ourselves, but there is no objective sense in which human life is important or cherished by nature. The average survival time of any mammalian species is only 500,000 years, and we humans have used up at least 50 per cent of them. With our lethal technologies, we may have used up quite a larger percentage than this; some experts propose that the threats from atomic weapons, microbes and out of control robotics and nanotechnologies imply that, in the absence of a rapid and substantial change in our values, civilisation has only a 50 per cent chance of lasting into the 22nd century.

There is nevertheless a perspective available from which human life matters, which can satisfy the need to belong to something greater than oneself and one's small sphere of personal concerns. Nearly every human being is able to philosophise, to reflect on the past and the future, and life as it is now, in a way that the other animals, as far as we know, cannot. The fact of belonging to the human species in the biological sense – being born, growing up, interacting cheerfully with others, loving some of them, producing offspring and dying to make way for the next generation – is a source of meaningfulness. Along with other living things, we participate in cycles of renewal and destruction. Contrary to the common perception of Epicureanism as a philosophy of selfishness and narrow self-interest, it is oriented to the whole of nature, especially – refracted through Lucretius's poetry – to living nature. We hand on the 'torch of life', as Lucretius calls it, to the next generation. The Epicurean understands that each living individual is part of a system that is ancient and perhaps perpetual. Although the universe may return to its original state – the quantum vacuum – and never emerge from it, many stars and planets will be born, develop, decline and disappear before that happens.

The beauty of living nature, the colours of autumn and the fantastic patterns of bare tree branches in winter, the appearance of plant life and the birth of young animals in springtime, testifies to nature's permanence as well as its impermanence. The drama of hailstorms and hurricanes and the quiet of the first heavy snowfall remind us that we feel and know that we are part of a vast system of worlds, all made from the same stuff, that is constantly evolving and changing and inventing new forms as well as preserving the old ones. The knowledge that death is inevitable and irreversible gives meaning to this life as the only life. The knowledge that other people's lives are their only lives makes us other than indifferent to the harms they suffer and desirous of not adding to their burdens.

To experience oneself as part of this system is to feel at once diminished – since our petty concerns about being liked and disliked, successful or ignored, rich or strapped for money to fulfil consumer ambitions, can come to feel trivial – and at the same time enlarged. The very fact of having been produced by mindless atoms and yet having a mind; of having been produced by blind forces and yet having direction and purpose, can seem miraculous. We become aware of our good fortune in existing in a vast and – for all practical, if not theoretical, purposes – otherwise lifeless universe.

The eating, drinking and mirthfulness of any social animal are not in every way different from our own. The Epicurean philosophers were more concerned to break down exalted human pride in our species than to puff it up by echoing the more usual views about human exceptionality. But as far as we know, we are the only species that can put pleasure in vitality and sadness over any death that is too abrupt a departure from the 'feast of life' into the wider context of life and beauty.

When, like Lucretius in Book VI, you are feeling especially pessimistic about the state of the world, it helps to visit a museum to marvel at what human beings can do when they are not engaged in conquest or wealth-acquisition, but only using their minds, hands and eyes to create objects of beauty. Their vases, pictures and even seemingly humble articles of everyday utility, such as woven baskets and embroidered slippers, can help to restore perspective and a faith in humanity, connecting us with what we can experience as absolute value outside ourselves. In these fabrications, the desire of the artist to excel through the use of his or her own powers and the wish to be useful and give pleasure to others have been fully realised.

15

SHOULD I BE A
STOIC INSTEAD?

[The Epicureans] argue with those who eliminate pains and tears and lamentations for the death of friends, and they say that the kind of freedom from pain which amounts to insensitivity is the result of another and greater bad thing, savagery or an unadulterated lust for fame and madness ...
Epicurus said this in lots of places.

Plutarch

[Epicurus says that] one must honour the noble, and the virtues and things like that, if they produce pleasure. But if they do not, one must bid them goodbye.

Athenaeus

To bring Epicureanism into ever sharper focus it is helpful to contrast the Epicurean perspective with the Stoic, especially as the latter is enjoying a revival in readership. Although the Stoics and the Epicureans were official opponents, there are areas of overlap. Both philosophies had epistemology, cosmology, political theory and ethics, and both connected their cosmologies to their accounts of the good life. Both philosophies were aimed at living well, with an untroubled mind and in accord with nature, even if Stoics and Epicureans did not attach the same meaning to those central concepts. Stoicism has its attractions, but it also has some real limitations that, to my mind, make Epicureanism more compelling.

THE STOIC SYSTEM

The Stoics of antiquity, whose main exponents were the Greek philosophers Zeno and Chrysippus and the Roman philosophers Seneca, Epictetus and Marcus Aurelius, regarded the world as under the guidance of providence and as permeated by a substance they called *pneuma*, a mixture of air and invisible fire, a form of vital breath, that gave life and order to everything. They were determinists who denied that anything happens by chance, though they recognised that many unknown causal factors influence a given outcome. Fate, therefore, has to be accepted and embraced. This did not, however, imply for them that effort, including moral effort, was futile. Everything in nature seeks to preserve itself, they thought, and reason allows us to form our own characters taking the orderly nature of the heavens as a model of stability and endurance. Stoic ethics is directed to, on the one hand, cultivating virtue, and on the other, reconciling oneself with the inevitable losses that human life entails.

The Stoics regarded moral authority as following from reason's recognition of the natural law. Order was immanent in nature, and moral norms such as care for children and respect for rulers were built into the nature of things. In this regard, they differed from the Epicureans who saw all justly imposed norms as based on community decisions as to what was conducive to the welfare of the group. Again, there were some issues on which there was agreement. Many Stoics were critics of slavery, which, like the Epicureans, they regarded as a conventional arrangement that conflicted with the natural equality of all humans. This was in opposition to the more usual view that some humans were naturally fit only to be slaves, which Aristotle represented forcefully and influentially, and which has persisted down to very recent times. However, they certainly had household servants in their community. Epicurus allowed slaves as well as women to take part in discussions of philosophy; the Stoics, as far as I know, did not, though Epictetus was a former slave.

The Stoics regarded the pleasant and the honourable as being in conflict. The Epicureans, they thought, failed to distinguish

Main Concepts	Stoics	Epicureans
Ontology	Pneuma	Atoms and void
Causality	Determinism, fate	Chance, free will
Purpose of ethics	Virtue	Freedom from harm
Source of moral authority	Natural law	Human agreement
Orientation	Universalist	Relativist
Emotions	Generally bad	Generally good
Family Life	Important	Inessential
Suicide	Recommended in difficult circumstances	Not recommended
Suffering	Inevitable	Minimisable
Pleasure	Generally bad	Generally good
Happiness	Freedom from all emotional disturbance	Freedom from anxiety and fear
Education	Develops human curiosity and capability	Undermines superstition
Warfare	Opportunity to display virtue	Motivated by greed and ambition

sufficiently between humans and other animals in supposing that all were alike in being ruled by pain and pleasure. The Epicureans emphasised the commonalities between humans and other animals, noting especially how similar maternal love, sexual passion and grief over the loss of loved ones were in both, while the Stoics, although they saw the drive for self-preservation as universal, emphasised the superior intellectual capabilities of humans and urged their followers to rise above their animal appetites and reactions. The previous chart summarises the two positions. It is a simplification that emphasises differences rather than similarities, and erases variations within the Stoic tradition, but it gives the general idea of the contrast.

TOO MUCH FORTITUDE?

The Stoic sees the world as orderly and rational, and human duties as objective and binding for everyone. In some respects, Stoicism is dignified, uplifting and indeed optimistic. But it has little place either for compassion or resistance to oppression in its philosophy, and it can seem blind to sources of satisfaction in human life.

The true Stoic, a determinist who maintains that everything that happens could not have failed to happen and that we must embrace our fates, does not grieve over any death. She reflects that the laws of nature make it inevitable that some children die of leukaemia, some middle-aged women of breast cancer and that old people are from time to time run over. School shootings, too, follow from the laws of nature ... a certain number of angry people; a certain number of available superweapons.

Toughness, rather than fragility, is a dominant motif in Stoicism, especially as it is revived today. Military personnel with an interest in philosophy or charged with teaching it are particularly attracted to it. While scholars may wish to point out that no Stoics were warmongers, and that some Stoics valued peace, there are obvious reasons why generals and soldiers are not drawn to Epicureanism. Where the Stoic demands fortitude in the face of physical danger and the tooth-gritting endurance of pain and captivity, the Epicurean asks only how to prevent warfare by limiting ambition, escaping religious and ideological fanaticism, and refraining from harm.

One of the most salient teachings of Stoicism was that the emotions are 'diseases' of the soul comparable to bodily illnesses. They are seen as disturbing our tranquillity and leading to obsessive, unproductive thinking. It is futile, the Stoics thought, to regret one's own former actions or to get upset about what other people are doing, since they cannot help behaving according to their characters. Even righteous anger could never be a force for good, the Stoic Seneca argued. An emotion, they thought, involves an interpretation of a situation affecting the self, and by gaining an objective perspective, the emotion will dissipate and peace of mind can be restored. Marcus Aurelius described the mind as an 'inner citadel' that external forces could never break down.

The best way of gaining perspective for the Stoic was to realise that one had not been singled out for an especially bad fate. Bad things are not uncommon and cannot always be anticipated or defended against. Because they were typically more involved in city life than the Epicureans, the Stoics were aware of the risks of political and financial life. Successful people arouse envy and breed competitors who want to take them down. Tyrants can be cruel and arbitrary, as Seneca learned under the Emperor Nero. One can be unjustly imprisoned on trumped-up charges or despoiled of property and sent into exile by powerful rivals.

The secret to living happily according to the Stoic moralist was to acknowledge that these things happen all the time, and not to become dependent on a certain level of wealth, authority or prestige. For the Stoics, there was no special mandate to live simply. You might enjoy wealth, power and prestige while you had it – as Seneca did – but you should make sure you are prepared to live without them. If things get too bad, killing yourself is the noble option. 'The door is open,' as they used to say.

The Stoics represent life as an ongoing series of trials and tribulations that test our fortitude. We are confronted with breakages and losses, with setbacks in our careers, financial downturns, painful illnesses, and betrayals by friends and lovers. Stoic ethics are concerned with self-defence, and the general recommendation they offered was to anticipate adversity so as not to be caught off-guard. According to the Stoic, to be troubled and upset is to allow yourself to be troubled and upset, and here you have a choice. You can cultivate inner calm and imperturbability. The Stoic can amend his will to suit the world and remain, in the words of Epictetus, 'sick and yet happy, in peril and yet happy, dying and yet happy, in exile and happy, in disgrace and happy'.

Although Epicurus claimed to be cheerful even on the last day of his life, the Epicurean frankly doubts that you always have a choice whether to be fearful, offended or overwhelmed by disappointment or grief. We don't suppose that the human body can face any degree of heat, cold or force and continue to live undisturbed. Why should we suppose that the human mind can survive any degree of shock and recover its equilibrium by applying mental effort alone? If the emotions are like diseases, are we not sometimes helpless to do anything but give our minds, like our bodies, time to heal through forgetfulness and distraction?

In any case, the Epicurean is not satisfied with the metaphor of the emotions as diseases of the soul. Suppose you could take a pill that would have the effect of your never feeling anxious, fearful, outraged, hurt, offended, jealous, ashamed and regretful, scornful or, for that matter, excited, passionate, hopeful, triumphant, compassionate or ambivalent? Would you be motivated to take such a pill in order to obtain tranquillity? People prescribed mood-blunting pills for their anxiety or manic-depressive illness often complain bitterly that life is unendurable in that state. And the fact that we seek out vicarious experiences, not only of the tender emotions but of anxiety and fear through literature and cinema shows that we value emotional experience as such when its long-term consequences are not painful. Feeling is a kind of knowing; it is only through our feelings that we know that we have been insulted, that we love someone, that danger lies ahead or that it is uncertain what next step we ought to take. To stifle emotions is to lose awareness of the world and engagement with it. Moreover, while some things must just be endured, because there is nothing we can do about it, human agency in response to emotional upsets can have a powerful remedial effect. Don't suffer in silence. Admit your hurt, confess your love and see what happens.

In the case of afflicting personal losses, as well as petty irritations, the Stoic maintains that we should take the view that such things happen every day. Epictetus advises: 'If, for example, you are fond of a specific ceramic cup, remind yourself that it is only ceramic cups in general of which you are fond. Then, if it breaks, you will not be disturbed. If you kiss your child, or your wife, say that you only kiss things which are human, and thus you will not be disturbed if either of them dies.'

To the Epicurean, the comparison between the breaking of a cup and the loss of a child to death is madness. In the latter case, you can only wear out your grief and, in time, look back fondly on your memories and hope for things to go better in the future.

WRAPPING UP

Ancient moral and political philosophy are resources for us today because they deal directly with real-life issues of work, love, professional ethics and political philosophy. At the same time, they place the discussion in a broader context that makes their stances and their advice-giving more grounded and less arbitrary than it would otherwise be. The return to ancient philosophy helps to fill in the large gap that exists between contemporary professional philosophy on the one hand and the advice columns and editorials of newspapers and blogs on the other. The former usually operates at a high level of abstraction, conjuring up thought experiments involving imaginary personal and political situations none of us will ever face. The latter, by contrast, even when it provides clear guidance, cannot show how its reasoning fits within a larger conception of nature and human life.

If you find the Stoic outlook more fitting to your own beliefs and experiences than the Epicurean, so be it. There are common elements in the two ancient philosophies that make each a source of value. Both are concerned with suffering as it occurs even in the midst of affluence. Both recognise that moral philosophy cannot just preach to people how best to live without explaining why that way is better than others.

Epicurean philosophy might be said to be based on the notion of the limit. First, there are natural limits to the lives of animals, people and material objects, to governments and to relation-ships. We preserve those we value as best we can from an

270

untimely end. Second, there are moral limits that we ought to observe and often fail to: limits on consumption, and on the domination and exploitation of other people and animals. By reconciling ourselves to natural limits and by taking moral limits seriously, we can spare ourselves – and future generations – fear, anxiety and suffering. At the same time, within these natural and moral limits, we can find ample, and often novel and unexpected, enjoyments in the material world and in the companionship of other people.

The inscription at the entrance of Epicurus's Garden reportedly read: 'Stranger, here you will do well to tarry; here our highest good is pleasure.' Defending the authentic Epicurus against those who tried to use him 'as a screen for their own vices', the Stoic Seneca advised a young friend as follows: 'Go to the Garden. The caretaker, a kindly host, will be ready for you; he will welcome you with barley-meal and serve you water also in abundance, with these words: "Have you not been well entertained?" "This garden," he says, "does not whet your appetite: it quenches it."'

A book can do no more than whet your appetite. But I hope you will take up the invitation to give Epicureanism a try.

BIBLIOGRAPHY AND SUGGESTIONS FOR FURTHER READING

Quotations in the text, whose sources are given chapter by chapter below, are taken from the following:

Titus Carus Lucretius, *On the Nature of Things (DRN)*, translated by Martin Ferguson Smith (Indianapolis: Hackett, 1994). Quoted by Book and line numbers.

Diogenes Laertius, *Lives of Eminent Philosophers (DL)*, translated by R. D. Hicks (Cambridge, MA: Harvard University Press, 1931). Quoted by Book and page number.

The Epicurus Reader (ER), translated and edited by Brad Inwood and L. P. Gerson, with an introduction by D. S. Hutchinson (Indianapolis: Hackett, 1994). Quoted by source and *ER* page number.

PREFACE

'[H]umans have dragged a body with a long hominid history into an overfed, malnourished, sedentary ...' Brandon Hidaka, 'Depression as a disease of modernity: explanations for increasing prevalence', *Journal of Affective Disorders*, 140:3 (2011): 205–214.

'[Epicurus] saw that almost everything that necessity demands for subsistence had already been provided for mortals ... he saw too that they possessed power, with wealth, honour and glory, and took pride in the good reputation of their children; and yet he found that, notwithstanding this prosperity, all of them privately had hearts ranked with anxiety ...' Lucretius, *DRN* VI: 9–14.

'By convention sweet, by convention bitter, by convention hot, by convention cold, by convention colour: but in reality, atoms and the void.' Democritus, Fragments, DL II: 75–9.

'Pleasure is our first and kindred good. It is the starting-point of every choice and of every aversion, and to it we come back, inasmuch as we make feeling the rule by which to judge of every good thing.' Epicurus, Letter to Menoeceus, DL X: 129.

1: BACK TO BASICS

'[T]he totality is made up of bodies and void ... Beyond these two things nothing can be conceived ... [A]mong bodies, some are compounds, and some are those things from which compounds have been made. And these are atomic and unchangeable ...' Epicurus, Letter to Herodotus, *ER* 6–7.

'[T]here are certain particles whose concurrences, movements, order, position and shapes produce fires; different combinations of them form things of different nature, but they themselves are unlike fire or any other thing ...' Lucretius, *DRN* I: 684–7.

'[A] finger ring is worn thin on the inside; the fall of water drop by drop hollows a stone ... we see the stone pavements of streets worn away by the feet of the crowd ...' Lucretius, *DRN* I: 312–13.

'[T]he same atoms ... constitute sky, sea, lands, rivers and sun: the same compose crops, trees and animals ...' Lucretius, *DRN* I: 820–1.

'Various sounds are continually floating through the air ... [W]hen we walk near the sea, a briny taste often makes its way into our mouth ... [F]rom all objects emanations flow away and are discharged in all directions on every side.' Lucretius, *DRN* IV: 221–6.

'[T]ime wholly destroys the things it wastes and sweeps away, and engulfs all their substance ...' Lucretius, *DRN* I: 225–6.

'Venus escort[s] each kind of creature back into the light of life.'
Lucretius, *DRN* I: 227–8.

'[N]o visible object ever suffers total destruction, since nature
renews one thing from another, and does not sanction the birth
of anything unless she receives the compensation of another's
death.' Lucretius, *DRN* I: 262–4.

2: How Did We Get Here?

'[F]rom time everlasting countless elements of things, impelled
by blows and by their own weight, have never ceased to move in
manifold ways, making all kinds of unions, and experimenting
with everything they could combine to create …' Lucretius,
DRN V: 422–6.

'[M]any species of animals must have perished and failed to
propagate and perpetuate their race. For every species that you
see breathing the breath of life has been protected and preserved
from the beginning of its existence either by cunning or by
courage or by speed.' Lucretius, *DRN* V: 854–9.

'I am extremely anxious that you should carefully avoid the
mistake of supposing that the lustrous eyes were created to
enable us to see; or that the tapering shins and thighs were
attached to the feet as a base to enable us to walk … All such
explanations are propounded preposterously with topsy-turvy
reasoning … Sight did not exist before the birth of the eyes …'
Lucretius, *DRN* IV: 823–36.

'One reviewer complained ... that there was nothing new in Darwin's "speculative" cosmogony. "It is at least as old," he said, "as Democritus and Epicurus, and has never been presented with more poetic beauty than by Lucretius".' Francis Bowen, Review of Charles Darwin, *On the Origin of Species by Means of Natural Selection*, North American Review 90 (1890): 474–506.

'Conscience, or a moral sense, would inevitably arise,' Charles Darwin, *The Descent of Man* (London: John Murray 1871), 71–2.

3: THE MATERIAL MIND

'[T]he spirit ... is born with the body, develops with it, and ... succumbs with it to the stress and strain of age.' Lucretius, *DRN* III: 455–6.

'[T]he spirit's interpenetration of the body through veins, flesh, sinews and bones is so complete that even the teeth are given a share in sensation, as is shown by toothache, or the twinge caused by icy water, or the crunching of rough grit concealed in a piece of bread.' Lucretius, *DRN* III: 686–90.

'... [T]the limbs become heavy; [the drunkards] reel about with staggering steps; the tongue drawls, the mind is sodden, the eyes swim ... [In an epileptic fit,] the spirit in every part of their frame is so distracted by the violence of the seizure that it surges and foams, just as the waves of the salt sea seethe beneath the furious force of the winds.' Lucretius, *DRN* III: 478–494.

'It is like the case of a wine whose bouquet has evaporated, or of a perfume whose exquisite scent has dispersed into the air, or of some object whose flavour has departed.' Lucretius, *DRN* III: 221–3.

'... what the neuroscientist Antonio Damasio calls "the feeling of what happens". Antonio Damasio, *The Feeling of What Happens: Body and Emotion in the Making of Consciousness* (New York: Harcourt, 1999).

4: THE STORY OF HUMANITY

'The human beings who lived on earth in those early days were far tougher than we are ... [T]hey were not easily affected by heat or cold or unaccustomed food or any physical malady. During many lustres of the sun revolving through the sky they lived random-roving lives like wild beasts ... What the sun and rains had given them, what the earth had spontaneously produced, were gifts rich enough to content their hearts.' Lucretius, *DRN* V: 925–38.

'[N]ever in those times did a single day consign to destruction many thousands of men marching between military standards; never did the boisterous billows of the ocean dash ships and sailors upon the rocks.' Lucretius, *DRN* V: 999–1001.

'Lucretius's reconstruction has been largely validated ...' See Bruce M. Knauft et al. 'Violence and Sociality in Human Evolution,' *Current Anthropology* 32:4 391–428.

'Later wealth was invented and gold discovered which robbed the strong and handsome of their prestige; for as a general rule ... people ... follow in the train of the rich.' Lucretius, *DRN* V: 1113–18.

'With bronze they tilled the soil, and with bronze they embroiled the billows of war, broadcast wide gaping wounds; and plundered flocks and fields; for everything unarmed and defenceless readily yielded to the armed.' Lucretius, *DRN* V: 1289–92.

[T]he situation sank to the lowest dregs of anarchy, with all seeking sovereignty and supremacy for themselves. At length some of them taught the others to create magistracies and established laws ... The reason why people were sick and tired of a life of violence was that each individual was prompted by anger to exact vengeance more cruelly than is now allowed by equitable laws.' Lucretius, *DRN* V: 1141–50.

'[H]uman beings never cease to labour vainly and fruitlessly, consuming their lives in groundless cares, evidently because they have not learned the proper limit to possession, and the extent to which real pleasure can increase.' Lucretius, *DRN* V: 1430–32.

5: ETHICS AND THE CARE OF THE SELF

'The cry of the flesh: not to be hungry, not to be thirsty, not to be cold. For if someone has these things and is confident of having them in the future, he might contend even with Zeus for happiness.' Epicurus, Vatican Collection of Epicurean Sayings, *ER* 38.

'I … do not even know what I should conceive the good to be, if I eliminate the pleasures of taste, and eliminate the pleasures of sex, and eliminate the pleasures of listening, and eliminate the pleasant motions caused in our vision by a sensible form.' Epicurus, reported by Athenaeus, *Deipnosophists*, ER 78.

'A *Cosmopolitan* article on how to treat yourself …' Robyn Munson, '9 Ways to Treat Yourself (That Aren't Wine)' *Cosmopolitan*, May 3, 2017. https://www.cosmopolitan.com/uk/worklife/a9200696/easy-ways-to-treat-yourself/.

'Although it is a cliché to say that the best things in life are free …' Daniel Kahneman, Alan B. Krueger, et al., 'A Survey Method for Characterising Daily Life Experience: The Day Reconstruction Method,' *Science* 306:5702 (2004): 1776–1780.

'[I]ncome and assets above a certain threshold have been found to have no bearing on subjective well-being …' Bruno Frey and Alois Stutzer, *Happiness and Economics: How the Economy and Institutions Affect Human Well-Being* (Princeton: Princeton University Press, 2001).

'Students of sociology, following Albert Hirschman,' Albert O. Hirschman, *Exit, Voice and Loyalty: Responses to Decline in Firms, Organisations and States* (Cambridge, MA: Harvard University Press, 1970).

'Of the things which wisdom provides for the blessedness of one's whole life, by far the greatest is the possession of friendship.' Epicurus, Vatican Sayings, *ER* 34.

6: MORALITY AND OTHER PEOPLE

'The justice of nature is a pledge of reciprocal usefulness …
neither to harm one another nor to be harmed … Justice was
not a thing in its own right, but [exists] in mutual dealings in
whatever places there [is] a pact about neither harming one
another nor being harmed.' Epicurus, Principal Doctrines, *ER*
35.

'It is impossible to live pleasantly without living prudently,
honourably and justly and impossible to live prudently,
honourably and justly without living pleasantly.' Epicurus,
Principal Doctrines, *ER* 32.

'[T]he selfishness and sadism of the Ik …' Colin Turnbull, *The
Mountain People* (New York: Simon and Schuster, 1972).

'[The terrors of Hell] do not exist and cannot exist anywhere at
all. But in life people are tortured by a fear of punishment as
cruel as their crimes.' Lucretius, *DRN* III: 1012–15.

7: BEWARE OF LOVE!

'So, in love, lovers are deluded by Venus with images: no matter
how intently they gaze at the beloved body, they cannot sate
their eyes; nor can they remove anything from the velvety limbs
that they explore with roving, uncertain hands.' Lucretius,
DRN IV: 1101–04.

'[P]erhaps his mistress has thrown out an ambiguous word and left it embedded in his passionate heart, where it burns like living fire; or perhaps he fancies that her eyes are wandering too freely, or that she is ogling some other man, while he detects in her face the trace of a smile.' Lucretius, *DRN* IV: 1137–40.

'[Who fear that the gods] have prevented them from ever being called father by sweet children ... condemned to live a life cursed with sterility.' Lucretius, *DRN* IV: 1232–5.

'[T]here are others like her; we have lived without her until now.' Lucretius, *DRN* IV: 1173–4.

'If you take away the chance to see and talk and spend time with [the beloved], then the passion of sexual love is dissolved.' Epicurus, Vatican Sayings, *ER* 36.

'[E]ven if male homosexuality has no "Darwinian" benefit for the individual, it may have one for his female relatives.' Andrea Camperio-Ciani, Francesca Corna and Claudio Capiluppi. 'Evidence for Maternally Inherited Factors Favouring Male Homosexuality and Promoting Female Fecundity.' *Proceedings of the Royal Society B: Biological Sciences* 271:1554 (2004): 2217–2221.

'[I]t is easier to avoid being lured into the traps of love than, once caught, to extricate yourself from the nets and burst the strong knots of Venus.' Lucretius, *DRN* IV: 1145–48.

'It might seem odd that ... you could harm someone by giving them, or just offering them, a cup of tea or a slice of cake.' The comparison is borrowed from the Thames Valley Police

YouTube tutorial on consent at: https://www.youtube.com/
watch?v=pZwvrxVavnQ.

8: Thinking About Death

'Death ... is nothing to us and does not affect us in the least,
now that the nature of the mind is understood to be mortal.
[When] body and soul, upon whose union our being depends,
are divorced, you may be sure that nothing at all will have the
power to affect us or awaken sensation in us, who shall not
then exist.' Lucretius, *DRN* III: 830–41.

'Why do you bemoan and beweep death? If your past life has
been a boon, and if not all your blessings have flowed
straight through you and run to waste like water poured into
a riddled vessel ... why, you fool, do you not retire from the
feast of life like a satisfied guest ...?' Lucretius, *DRN* III:
934–9.

'When we exist, death is not yet present, and when death is
present, then we do not exist.' Epicurus, Letter to Menoeceus,
ER 78.

'A recent article in the British medical journal *The Lancet*
estimates that, worldwide, 45 per cent of the dying ...
experience severe suffering.' 'A sea of suffering', *The Lancet* 391
(2018):1465.

'Never again ... will your household receive you with joy; never
again will the best of wives welcome you home; never again will
your dear children race for the prize of your first kisses and

touch your heart with pleasure too profound for words.'
Lucretius, *DRN* III: 894–8.

'Stop snivelling, you dolt ... You had full use of all the precious
things of life before you reached this senile state ... Because you
continually crave what is not present and scorn what is, your
life has slipped away from you incomplete and unenjoyed ...
Quick then, discard all behaviour unsuited to your age and with
equanimity yield to your years; for yield you must.' Lucretius,
DRN III: 955–62.

'It is absurd to pursue death because you are weary of life when
you have made death worth pursuing by your way of life.'
Epicurus, reported by Seneca, Letter 24 to Lucilius, *ER* 103.

9: WHAT IS REAL?

'A property is what cannot under any circumstances be severed
and separated from a body ... such is the relationship of
heaviness to rocks, heat to fire, liquidity to water ... On the
other hand, to slavery, poverty and wealth, freedom, war,
concord, and all other things whose coming and going does not
impair the essential nature of a thing, we ... apply the
appropriate term accidents.' Lucretius, *DRN* I: 451–8.

'[A]ll events without exception have, unlike matter, no
independent existence.' Lucretius, *DRN* I: 478–9.

'... the terrifying illusion of hearing and seeing face to face
people who are dead, and whose bones are embosomed in the
earth'. Lucretius, *DRN* I: 134–5.

'Many careful sociological studies will confirm that their perceptions are accurate.' Elisabeth Kneebone, Cary Nadeau and A. Berube, 'The Re-Emergence of Concentrated Poverty: Metropolitan Trends in the 2000s', Brookings Institution Metropolitan Policy Program Report (2011), https://community-wealth.org/sites/clone.community-wealth.org/files/downloads/paper-kneebone-nadeau-berube.pdf.

'[W]hat has worsened or failed to improve are the policies governing housing, zoning and development in the cities and suburbs.' See Alana Semuels, 'Good School, Rich School; Bad School, Poor School', *The Atlantic*, 25 August 2016, https://www.theatlantic.com/business/archive/2016/08/property-taxes-and-unequal-schools/497333/.

10: WHAT CAN WE KNOW?

'[W]e must attend to present feelings and to sense perceptions, whether those of mankind in general or those peculiar to the individual, and also attend to all the clear evidence available, as given by each of the standards of truth.' Epicurus, Letter to Herodotus, DL X: 82.

'[F]leecy sheep crop the luxuriant pasture and inch forward wherever the tempting grass, pearled with fresh dew, summons them, while their lambs, replete with food, gambol and gently butt. Yet to us in the distance, the whole scene seems indistinct, appearing only as a motionless white blur on the green of the hill.' Lucretius, *DRN* II: 317–22.

'The number of people living in US ghettos and slums has nearly doubled since 2000.' Paul A. Jargowsky, 'The Architecture of Segregation: Civil Unrest, the Concentration of Poverty and Public Policy', *The Century Foundation* 7 (2015).

'... as the philosopher Bas Van Fraassen maintains, a stance I can *choose*, for good philosophical reasons, to adopt.' Bas Van Fraassen, *The Empirical Stance* (New Haven: Yale University Press, 2002).

'[W]hen people assert that the rape [of Helen] and the subjugation of the people of Troy in war are facts, beware of possibly being trapped by them into an acknowledgement that these events have an independent existence, simply because those generations of human beings, of whom they were accidents, have been swept away beyond recall ...' Lucretius, *DRN* I: 465–8.

11: Science and Scepticism

'There would be no advantage in providing security against our fellow men, so long as we were alarmed by occurrences over our heads or beneath the earth or in general by what happens in the boundless universe.' Epicurus, Principal Doctrines, DL X: 143.

'[I]n the study of nature, we must not conform to empty assumptions and arbitrary laws, but follow the promptings of the facts; for our life has no need now of unreason and false opinion.' Epicurus, DL X: 87.

'Hallowed formulas, such as the injunction to drink eight glasses of water a day, turn out to be mythical inventions.' Heinz Valtin and Sheila A. Gorman, '"Drink at least eight glasses of water a day." Really? Is there scientific evidence for "8 x 8"?' *American Journal of Physiology-Regulatory, Integrative and Comparative Physiology*, 283:5 (2002):993–1004.

'Industry-sponsored studies of efficacy and safety have been put in doubt by more independent investigators.' See John Peterson Myers, et al. 'Concerns over Use of Glyphosate-Based Herbicides and Risks Associated with Exposures: A Consensus Statement.' *Environmental Health* 15 (2016): 19.

'The researcher most credited for recommending margarine ...' Ancel Keys, *Seven Countries. A multivariate analysis of death and coronary heart disease* (Cambridge: Harvard University Press, 1980).

'But heart attacks among people who substituted margarine for butter actually increased.' M. W. Gillman, L. A. Cupples, D. Gagnon, B. E. Millen, R. C. Ellison and W. P. Castelli, 'Margarine intake and subsequent coronary heart disease in men.' *Epidemiology* 8: 2 (1987): 144–149.

'The sugar industry had seized on his published claims and provided financial incentives to several Harvard University researchers ...' C. E. Kearns, L. A. Schmidt, S. A. Glantz, 'The Sugar Industry and Coronary Heart Disease Research: A Historical Analysis of Internal Industry Documents.' *JAMA Intern Med.* 176:11 (2016):1680–1685.

'Reducing cholesterol levels, for example, has a protective effect against cardiovascular disease but unfortunately does not lead to a longer life.' R. DuBroff and M. de Lorgeril, 'Cholesterol Confusion and Statin Controversy,' *World Journal of Cardiology.* 7:7 (2015):404–409.

'... only about 20 per cent of recently surveyed people at all educational levels, from high-school graduates to those with postgraduate degrees, follows the scientific consensus.' ews. gallup.com/poll/210956/belief-creationist-view-humans-new-low.aspx.

12: Social Justice for an Epicurean World

'Kings began to build cities and to choose sites for citadels to be strongholds and places of refuge for themselves; and they distributed gifts of flocks and fields to individuals according to their beauty, strength and intellect ... Later wealth was invented and gold discovered ... [T]he situation sank to the lowest dregs of anarchy, with all seeking sovereignty and supremacy for themselves.' Lucretius, *DRN* V: 1108–1142.

'A free life cannot acquire great wealth, because the task is not easy without slavery to the mob or those in power ... And if [one] does somehow achieve great wealth, one could easily share this out in order to obtain the good will of one's neighbours.' Epicurus, Vatican Sayings, *ER* 39.

'To exist in a market economy,' Sahlins said, 'is to live a double tragedy, beginning in inadequacy and ending in desperation.'

Marshall Sahlins, Discussion II in *Man the Hunter*, ed. Richard B. Lee and Irven De Vore (Chicago: Aldine, 1968) 86.

'Engels believed that Epicureanism's contributions to enlightenment were its commitment to "the original goodness and equal intellectual endowment of men, the omnipotence of experience, habit and education, and the influence of environment on man, the great significance of industry, [and] the justification of enjoyment."' 'The Holy Family or Critique of Critical Criticism', tr. in Karl Marx and Friedrich Engels, *On Religion* (Atlanta: Scholars Press, 1982) 67.

'[F]or each instance of successful self-defence or justifiable homicide using a gun, there were twenty-two cases of assault or criminal homicide, unintentional homicide, suicide and attempted suicide using a gun.' Arthur L. Kellermann, et al., 'Injuries and Deaths Due to Firearms in the Home', in *Journal of Trauma: Injury, Infection and Critical Care*, 45: 2 (1998), https://www.scientificamerican.com/article/more-guns-do-not-stop-more-crimes-evidence-shows/.

'[I]n problem solving, creativity, general intelligence and task persistence, there are no significant differences between the genders.' Eleanor Maccoby and Carol Jacklin, *The Psychology of Sex Differences* (Stanford: Stanford University Press, 1978) 61.

'What differences does it make whether it is a wife or a mother, when a man has to guard against Eve in every woman.' Saint Augustine, Letter 243. In vol. 5 of Saint Augustine, *Letters*, tr. Sister Wilfrid Parsons (New York: Catholic University of America Press, 1956) 225.

'Does a slave possess any other excellence, besides his merits as a tool and a servant ... [Nearly the same question] is raised about the woman and the child.' Aristotle, *Politics* 1259b, in *Complete Works*, 2 vols., ed. Jonathan Barnes (Princeton, Princeton University Press, 1984, II: 1991).

'In general outline justice is the same for everyone ... But ... if someone passes a law and it does not turn out to be in accord with what is useful in mutual associations, this no longer possesses the nature of justice.' Epicurus, Principal Doctrines, *ER* 35.

13: Religion From an Epicurean Perspective

'First believe that God is a living being immortal and blessed, according to the notion of a god indicated by the common sense of mankind ... For verily, there are gods, and the knowledge of them is manifest; but they are not such as the multitude believe ...' Epicurus, Letter to Menoeceus, DL X: 123.

'[Y]ou may perhaps imagine that you are starting on the principles of an irreligious philosophy [Epicurus's] and setting out on a path of wickedness. But in fact more often it is that very superstition that has perpetrated wicked and irreligious deeds.' Lucretius, *DRN* I: 80–4.

'[E]ven in remote antiquity, the minds of mortals were visited in waking life, and still more in sleep, by visions of divine figures of matchless beauty and stupendous stature ... They took refuge in ascribing everything to the gods and in supposing that

290

everything happened in obedience to their will.' Lucretius, *DRN* V: 1169–87.

'What sorrows did they prepare for themselves, what wounds for us, what tears for generations to come!' Lucretius, *DRN* V: 1196–7.

'Consider how numerous are the fantasies they can invent, capable of confounding your calculated plan of life and clouding all your fortunes with fear.' Lucretius, *DRN* I: 104–6.

14: THE MEANINGFUL LIFE

'And so human beings never cease to labour vainly and fruitlessly, consuming their lives in groundless cares, evidently because they have not learned the proper limit to possession … And it is this ignorance that has gradually carried life out into the deep sea and has stirred up from the depths the mighty boiling billows of war.' Lucretius, *DRN* V: 1430–35.

'He who has learned the limits of life knows that it is easy to provide that which removes the feeling of pain owing to want and makes one's whole life perfect. So there is no need for things which involve struggle.' Epicurus, *ER* 34.

'We do not assess the absolute value of the existence of the world by reference to [human] well-being or enjoyment (whether bodily or intellectual) – in a word, happiness.' Kant, *Critique of Judgement*, tr. Werner S. Pluhar (Indianapolis: Hackett, 1987) V 442.

'Navigation, agriculture, city walls, laws, arms, roads, clothing and all other practical inventions, as well as every one of life's rewards and refinements, poems, pictures and polished statues of exquisite workmanship ... People saw one thing after another become clear in their minds until each art reached the peak of perfection.' Lucretius, *DRN* V: 1448–57.

'... their languid limbs half dead, caked with filth, covered with rags ...' Lucretius, *DRN* VI: 1268–70.

15: Should I Be a Stoic Instead?

'[The Epicureans] argue with those who eliminate pains and tears and lamentations for the deaths of friends, and they say that the kind of freedom from pain which amounts to insensitivity is the result of another and greater bad thing, savagery or an unadulterated lust for fame and madness ... Epicurus said this in lots of places.' Plutarch, A Pleasant Life, *ER* 79.

'[Epicurus says,] One must honour the noble, and the virtues, and things like that, *if* they produce pleasure. But if they do not, one must bid them goodbye.' Athenaeus, *Deipnosophists*, *ER* 78.

'If, for example, you are fond of a specific ceramic cup, remind yourself that it is only ceramic cups in general of which you are fond. Then, if it breaks, you will not be disturbed. If you kiss your child, or your wife, say that you only kiss things which are human, and thus you will not be disturbed if either of them dies.' Epictetus, *Enchiridion* 3, tr. Elizabeth Carter, CreateSpace Independent Publishing Platform, 2017, 9.

'Stranger, here you will do well to tarry; here our highest good is pleasure.' Epicurus, reported by Lucius Annaeus Seneca, Letter 21 to Lucilius in *Letters*, 3 vols. tr. Richard Mott Gunmere (Cambridge MA: Harvard University Press) I:147.

SUGGESTIONS FOR FURTHER READING

For further reading, there are excellent blogs and discussion groups devoted to Epicureanism, for example http://www. epicurus.net/index.html.

For the reader who would like to investigate the Epicurean tradition further, the following are a good start, and all have useful bibliographies of their own:

Clay, Diskin, *Lucretius and Epicurus* (Ithaca: Cornell University Press, 1983).

Greenblatt, Stephen, *The Swerve* (NY: Norton, 2012).

Konstan, David, *'A Life Worthy of the Gods': The Materialist Psychology of Epicurus* (Las Vegas: Parmenides Publishing, 2008).

Warren, James, *Facing Death: Epicurus and his Critics* (Oxford: Clarendon Press, 2004).

Wilson, Catherine, *Epicureanism at the Origins of Modernity* (Oxford: Clarendon Press, 2008).

Credit: Nick Coleman

Catherine Wilson received her PhD in philosophy from Princeton University and has taught at universities in the United States, Canada, and Europe. She has published more than one hundred research papers and eight books, including *A Very Short Introduction to Epicureanism* and *Metaethics from a First-Person Standpoint*. She has two children and lives in New York City, where she is currently visiting presidential professor of philosophy at the Graduate Center at CUNY.

ACKNOWLEDGEMENTS

I am grateful to my agent, Adam Gauntlett, and my editors, Zoe Berville and T. J. Kelleher, who launched this project and who have seen it through with exemplary helpfulness. Their advice has been welcome at every stage. Special thanks are due as well to Eva, whose sharp eye and good judgment improved many passages, and to David for sharing his useful knowledge. This book is dedicated to my mother, Martha Wilson. Her Epicurean sense for friendship and gracious living – with 'moderation in all things' – frames both a long scientific career and an active commitment to peace and social justice.